## ★ 1947

**Jan** — Fox contract renewed for another six months

**Feb** — Makes her first film appearance in *Scudda-Hoo! Scudda-Hey!*

**Aug** — Fox contract not renewed

**Dec** — Her first film to be released is *Dangerous Years*, four months before *Scudda-Hoo! Scudda-Hey!*

## ★ 1948

**Mar 9** — Signs contract with Columbia Pictures

**Sept 8** — Columbia contract not renewed

**Dec 31** — Meets Johnny Hyde who agrees to promote her

## ★ 1949

**May 27** — Poses for nude calendar shots with photographer Tom Kelley

**Oct** — Signs with MGM for role in *The Asphalt Jungle* which proves a breakthrough for her

## ★ 1950

**Apr** — Another important role, this time in *All About Eve*

**Dec 18** — Johnny Hyde dies, shortly after securing a long-term contract with Fox

**Sept** — First major feature in a national magazine, *Collier's*

## ★ 1952

**Mar** — First date with baseball star Joe DiMaggio

**Mar 13** — Scandal breaks over the nude calendar shoot

**Apr 7** — First cover for *Life* magazine

**June 1** — Is given key part in *Gentlemen Prefer Blondes*

**Sept** — Appears as Grand Marshal in the Miss America parade

## ★ 1953

**Jan 21** — Achieves stardom with the release of *Niagara*

**June 26** — With *Gentlemen Prefer Blondes* co-star Jane Russell, Marilyn leaves her hand prints outside Grauman's Chinese Theater on Hollywood Boulevard

**Sept 13** — TV debut on *The Jack Benny Show*

**Nov 4** — Premiere of *How To Marry A Millionaire*

# Marilyn
# handbook

# Marilyn handbook

## Mike Evans

MQP

MQ Publications Ltd

# Marilyn

# Introduction

There was a time when "star" really meant something. Applied to film stars, the term was particularly apt. Like gazing at the constellations of the night sky, cinema audiences literally looked up at them, there on the silver screen, the world around in darkness. More importantly, as with the heavenly lights that had fascinated man since the dawn of time, they seemed to be untouchable.

The term gradually became overused, of course, and as a result devalued—so much so that by the end of the 1960s the "superstar" had arrived, followed a few years later by the "mega-star," each time the words meaning less, the subjects more ordinary.

Marilyn Monroe was the last of the great stars in that classic sense of the word. Her career, which flowered, reached its peak, and ended between the early 1950s and early 1960s, spanned a time of great change in the cinema industry and the world at large. It was a time when screen actors as seemingly untouchable idols were becoming a thing of the past, due in part to the emergence of more "realistic" styles of film and the new intimacy of television.

This naturalism, epitomized in Europe by the French New Wave cinema, was personified in America by the Method school—Brando, Clift, Newman, and directors such as Elia Kazan—which Marilyn aspired to as her acting ambitions became more focused.

In her first starring roles in the early fifties she represented the ultimate blonde bombshell, whether the sassy femme fatale of *Niagara* or the kooky Lorelei Lee of *Gentlemen Prefer Blondes*.

But by 1961's *The Misfits* she was just that, a more mature beauty whose va-va-voom trademarks—the platinum blonde hair, hour-glass figure, skimpy dresses—weren't quite right any more. The conflict in style was perfect for the part that husband,

Arthur Miller, had written for her, but uncomfortably appropriate to the real-life Marilyn as well.

Hers was a life that was in many ways unfulfilled, professionally and privately. Certainly the natural talent in front of the camera that those around her acknowledged—albeit begrudgingly in many cases—was never given the opportunity to develop as it might have done. A career of lackluster or at best lightweight films was occasionally interrupted by more substantial vehicles: *Don't Bother To Knock*, *Niagara*, *The Seven Year Itch*, *Bus Stop*, *Some Like It Hot* immediately spring to mind, and of course the much-maligned *Misfits*. But even in the frothy romantic comedies that formed much of her starring output, when she appeared on screen it was hard to take your eyes off her—her presence eclipsing those around her with what can only be described as sheer charisma.

Likewise in her personal life, despite her rags-to-riches success it was a story of short-lived relationships and broken dreams. None of her three marriages lasted more than four years, and she could virtually count truly loyal, long-term friends on the fingers of two hands—her second husband Joe DiMaggio, although they were married for less than two years, among them.

The first indication that Marilyn was destined for more than her unquestioned star status came with her tragic death, when the posthumous spotlight—focused initially on the circumstances of her passing—turned her life into legend and her image into icon. And that spotlight hasn't moved off Marilyn Monroe in more than forty years.

**Note: All quotations are from Marilyn Monroe, unless otherwise indicated.**

## chapter 1

# Orphan child, teenage bride

# "Like a dream walking" 1926–46

Marilyn Monroe was born Norma Jeane Mortenson on June 1, 1926, at the Los Angeles General Hospital, the third child of Gladys Pearl Baker, née Monroe (May 25, 1900–March 11, 1984). Her birth certificate gave her father's name as Mortenson, after Edward Mortenson who was married to Gladys a couple of years previous to the birth, but she was later baptized as Norma Jeane (the "e" later often dropped by Marilyn and subsequent biographers) Baker. Despite using the registered name for official purposes, Marilyn later refuted that Mortenson was her father.

In fact Gladys didn't actually divorce Mortenson for another two years, when he reappeared in Los Angeles, having disappeared to San Francisco on a motorbike just months after their marriage. In at least one interview Marilyn claimed that her real father lived in the same apartment building as her mother, and left during the pregnancy. The individual she referred to was almost certainly Stanley Gifford, a divorced salesman working for the same film laboratory, Consolidated Film Industries, where Gladys was head negative cutter.

After increasing bouts of depression, Gladys was committed to Norwalk State Asylum—diagnosed as a paranoid schizophrenic—when Norma Jeane was just eight years old, the child being made ward of Gladys's friend and work colleague, Grace McKee. At this stage McKee, who was single, was unable to take her in on a permanent basis, and she lived with various foster parents including the Bolanders, a well-educated English couple, and the well-to-do Giffens who wanted to adopt her but had to move to Mississippi. In September 1935, McKee arranged for her to enter the orphanage of the Los Angeles Orphans Home Society.

Two years later Grace McKee married Erwin "Doc" Goddard, and was able to look after Norma Jeane on a more regular basis. Eventually Grace Goddard moved (with Norma and her other "adopted daughter" Eleanor, known as Bebe) into her husband's house in the suburb of Van Nuys. Although, initially, Norma Jeane was still moved between foster homes and orphan institutions, Grace Goddard was a formative influence on the now eleven-year-old.

An even greater influence, certainly on an emotional level, was Grace Goddard's aunt, Ana Lower, who Norma Jeane moved in with in 1941. The sixty-year-old widow adored the girl, this being reciprocated from 1938 through to Aunt Ana's death in 1948. As a Christian Scientist, Ana took Norma Jeane to church every Sunday, and the impression it left was in marked contrast to the hedonism she would be surrounded by in later life, though how much of its teaching Marilyn took on board is hard to say. But she treasured the copy of *Science and Health with Key to the Scriptures* by Christian Science founder Mary Baker Eddy which Ana gave her before her death, inscribed thus: "Norma dear, read this book. I do not leave you much except my love, but not even death can diminish that; nor will death ever take me far away from you."

In 1938 Norma Jeane entered Emerson Junior High, where one of her first regular boyfriends a couple of years later was Chuck Moran. She was to recall how they went dancing at Ocean Pier Park between Venice and Santa Monica, west of LA:

"We danced until we thought we'd drop, and then when we headed outside for a Coca-Cola and a walk in the cool breeze, Chuckie let me know he wanted more than just a dance partner. Suddenly his hands were everywhere! … Poor Chuck, all he got was tired feet and a fight with me."

The Goddards' neighbors in Van Nuys were the Doughertys, whose eldest son Jimmy was a star in the football team and student body at Van Nuys High school, which Norma attended after Emerson. When Grace and Doc had to move to West Virginia on account of Doc's work, they couldn't afford to take sixteen-year-old Norma Jeane with them, so it was arranged that she and the twenty-one-year-old Jimmy—who had been dating for about six months—should get married.

They were wed on June 19, 1942. "She was a sweet, generous and religious girl," Jimmy later recalled. "She liked to be cuddled." By all accounts Norma Jeane loved Jimmy, and they were happy together—"We fished, hunted, rode horses, went to movies and enjoyed family gatherings where there was music, good food, and lots of laughter"—until he joined the Merchant Marines and was sent to the South Pacific in 1944.

Norma Jeane, meanwhile, took a job (arranged by her mother-in-law, Ethel Dougherty, who worked there as a nurse) on the assembly line at the Radio Plane Company in Burbank. She earned twenty dollars a week for ten hours' work a day, spraying foul-smelling varnish on aircraft fuselage fabric. But working in the "dope room," as it was called, was to prove a catalyst in Norma Jeane's life.

Ordered by his commanding officer (the actor and later US President, Ronald Reagan) to take some "morally uplifting snapshots of pretty girls" working in the war effort, for the army magazine *Yank*, photographer David Conover spotted Norma Jeane at the factory. Immediately struck by her appearance, he used her for the shoot, and started to put other modeling work her way. At five dollars an hour it was work she couldn't turn down, and soon, via Conover, the name "Norma Jeane Dougherty" was on the books of the influential Blue Book Modeling Agency.

As the modeling took off from late 1945 the strain began to show on her marriage to Jim Dougherty, who was only home for short periods at a time, during which she was clearly preoccupied with her new-found role as a pin-up, and potential fame and fortune. A photo shoot with the photographer André de Dienes ended in a short-lived affair, followed by work with other famous photographers that put her on magazine covers for the first time.

It became clear that a life-defining choice had to be made: between her floundering marriage and her burgeoning career. In June 1946 she filed for divorce from Jimmy Dougherty, and on July 17 had her first audition with a film studio, at 20th Century Fox.

There was a luminous quality to her face, a fragility combined with astonishing vibrancy.

**David Conover, photographer**

My mother's first husband was named Baker. Her second was Mortenson. But she'd divorced both of them by the time I was born.

*Right:* **Norma Jeane Mortenson, age six months**

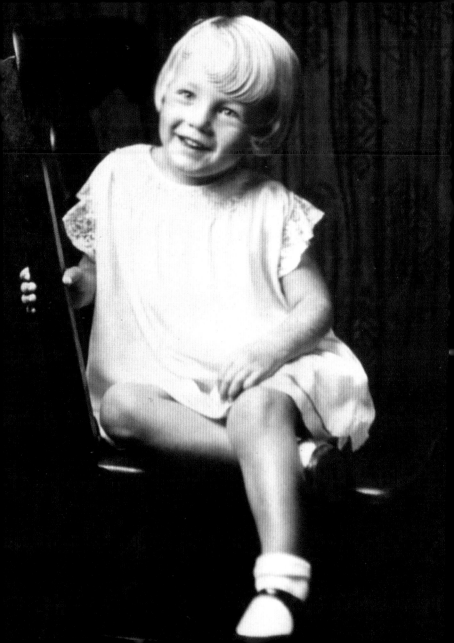

No one ever told me I was pretty when
I was a little girl; all little girls should be told
they are pretty even if they're not.

*Left:* **Norma Jeane, 1929**
Norma Jeane Baker at three years old, already relaxed in front of the camera, as she would be for the rest of her life.

*Next page:* **Santa Monica, 1928**
Marilyn Monroe's mother Gladys Monroe Baker (left) with a tearful two-year-old Norma Jeane at Santa Monica beach, west of Los Angeles, 1928.

# Teenage bride

Norma Jeane Baker's short courtship and swift marriage to former next-door-neighbor Jim Dougherty was unusual, if only because it was conceived and arranged by Grace Goddard and, to a lesser degree, Grace's Aunt Ana Lower and Jim's mother, Ethel.

The Dougherty boy who had shone at Van Nuys High as a football player was, by 1940, the twenty-year-old Dougherty man who worked the night shift at Lockheed Aircraft, drove a cool blue Ford coupé and dated a succession of local girls including Doris Drennan, the Santa Barbara Festival Queen. Eligible indeed!

The first contact he had with Norma Jeane was when his mother Ethel and Grace Goddard asked him to drive the fifteen-year-old and her "sister" Bebe home from school each day—the Goddards having moved out of the Van Nuys area by that time. Least pleased was his girlfriend, the Santa Barbara beauty, who complained about him "hauling a little sexpot like that" around in his car.

Next in what was now a grand plan on Grace Goddard's part was to ask Jim to escort the youngster to the Christmas dance held by Doc Goddard's place of work, Adel Precision Products. And although at first he feared he was cradle-snatching, after dancing (especially in the slow numbers!) with the eager teenager five years his junior, Dougherty realized this was a young woman pressing herself against him, and an attractive one at that.

After that, they were dating steadily by March 1942, and engaged in May to be married in June 1942. Their courtship was aided and abetted by Grace—she would even pay for them to go to the movies. However, when she and Doc Goddard announced they were having to move east, it was Ethel Dougherty who mooted to

her son that the way to "rescue" Norma Jeane from a return to an orphanage—Aunt Ana being too ill to look after her at this point—might be for them to get married.

The couple were married at 8:30 in the evening on Friday, June 19, 1942, at a ceremony conducted by the Reverend Benjamin Lingenfelder, held at the home of Mr. and Mrs. Chester Howell (friends of Grace's) at 432 South Bentley Avenue, West Los Angeles. A friend of Norma Jeane's from University High—the final school she attended—was matron of honor, and Jim's cousin Marion was best man. The party—absent from which was Norma Jeane's mother, now institutionalized—then moved on to a nearby Italian restaurant, the Florentine Gardens, for a modest reception; the only memorable event on record seems to have been when a waiter spilled tomato soup on the bridegroom's white (rented) tuxedo jacket.

For the first six months of married life, the Doughertys lived in a one-room rented cabin in Sherman Oaks, later to move temporarily back to the Archwood Street, Van Nuys house of Jim's parents who had moved for a short while out of LA. Jim was still at Lockheed, where a workmate was the actor (and Marilyn's co-star) to be, Robert Mitchum. An anecdotal encounter between the two centered on the cold egg sandwich Norma Jeane made for Jim every day: Mitchum asked "Your old lady makes you the same sandwich every day?" to which Jim replied "You ought to see my old lady!" Mitchum answered, "I hope she looks better than your egg sandwich."

Jim, however, always socially "one of the boys," got restless as various buddies went overseas on military service. Norma Jeane, naturally, was anxious he should stay at home—which he could, working in the aircraft industry—so he compromised by enlisting in the Merchant Marines in 1943. He was stationed at the peacetime holiday resort island of Catalina, now a service training base, his wife joining him toward the end of the year. But their time at Catalina marked the first strains in their relationship, brought to a head, according to Dougherty, by his young wife's growing awareness of the dramatic effect she could have on men in this predominantly male military environment.

**... wearing a tight white blouse and tight white shorts, with a ribbon in her hair for a touch of color, it was like a dream walking down the street.**

**Jim Dougherty**

Although it never got past flirting, Jim was increasingly jealous of the attention Norma Jeane attracted, be it weight lifting at the gym, casually flirting at dances, or just walking the walk down the midday main street. He was probably relieved (and she, too, for other reasons) when in 1944 he was posted to the Far East and she moved back to LA to live with his mother Ethel in North Hollywood.

Things didn't get any easier, however. It was at the Radio Plane factory, where Ethel worked and had secured her daughter-in-law a job, that Norma Jeane was first photographed for a magazine, an assignment that quickly led to full-time glamour modeling. At first, the mainly absent Dougherty didn't see a problem in this— "I thought it was easier than working at Radio Plane"—but by the middle of 1946 Norma Jeane, now appearing in dozens of pinup magazines, had been involved in more than one affair with her photographers, and was poised to make the inevitable choice between an increasingly doomed marriage and potentially stellar career. She chose the latter, and the couple were divorced in September 1946.

# We could spend hours in the evening on our porch, planning our future after the war.

## Jim Dougherty on life in Catalina

*Left:* **Mr and Mrs James Dougherty, 1943**

Norma Jeane Dougherty with her husband Jim during his wartime service in the Merchant Marines, not long after he had enlisted.

Norma Jeane told me that she was an illegitimate child ... and of course it made no difference to me. The fact that she was illegitimate, I think just made her that much more beautiful.

**Jim Dougherty**

*Right:* **Norma Jeane, 1944**

Jim Dougherty conceded that the person he knew was Norma Jeane Baker, not the later sex symbol: "I never looked at Marilyn as Norma Jeane. To me there were two people, and I didn't know Marilyn."

# Pinup girl

Although David Conover's later memoir of his association with Marilyn is considered to be riddled with inaccuracy and exaggeration, including mention of sexual encounters which may or may not have taken place, his role in introducing her to the camera is beyond dispute. Nevertheless, had he not chosen her for the factory floor shoot at Radio Plane it's equally certain she would have followed the path he described, one way or another.

**Norma Jeane wants to be a movie star. (Seems everybody does these days—ha!) I told her she would have to be a model first, and to think about it.**

**David Conover**

Conover had been assigned to the Army's 1st Motion Picture Unit, nicknamed "Fort Roach" on account of it being based in the Hal Roach Studio in Culver City. Commanding Officer Ronald Reagan wanted some pictures of women on the assembly line engaged in the war effort, but not regular documentary shots of anonymous-looking females in overalls, more something the troops who read the service magazine *Yank* would enjoy—and "commercial" enough to be used in civilian publications.

David Conover couldn't believe his luck when he spied Norma Jeane working in the dope room, spray can in hand. Accompanied by the factory foreman, they moved to a more appropriate location where the small engines for the radio-controlled target aircraft were assembled. Norma Jeane's first ever "glamour" shot showed her smiling at the camera holding an airplane propeller. This is one of a handful of surviving shots from the session, along with a couple more taken outside the plant. But Conover was hooked on his new find, and she on being in front of that camera.

Conover took more pictures of his discovery over the subsequent weeks, at the same time recommending her to fellow photographers. So began a love affair with the camera which would define the rest of her life. From the start self-critical to the point of nervousness, she would suddenly light up, "courting the lens" as more than one observer put it, when the camera was about to click. So it was to be a few years later on the movie set—stage fright would set in, lines fumbled, entrances fudged, but when the cameras rolled she simply glowed.

The Blue Book Modeling Agency, which Marilyn was introduced to by Conover in August 1945, was founded and run by a rather stern-mannered and matronly Englishwoman, Emmeline Snively. Like dozens of other agencies in the city, it reflected the needs of the hundreds of aspiring models in Los Angeles, most of whom saw modeling as the first step to an acting career in the movies. Based on Sunset Boulevard, it was as Hollywood as an agency could be for the inexperienced but increasingly screen-struck Norma Jeane.

After a few not particularly successful jobs modeling clothes—where Marilyn later recalled they seemed to be looking at her rather than the garments—for catalog work and a Hollywood fashion show, Snively started to send her to pose for magazine editors and what we would today call "glamour" photographers. By early 1946, Norma Jeane, sometimes credited as "Jean Norman," had appeared on more than thirty covers for men's magazines such as *Glamorous Models*, *Pageant*, *Laff*, *Click* and *See*.

Before the December 1953 debut of *Playboy* (which featured Marilyn on its cover), with its increasingly revealing glamour shots, "pinup" magazines on both sides of the Atlantic were considered seedy if not downright pornographic by polite society, though usually completely innocuous by today's standards. The names said it all—*Peek, Glance*, *Foto Parade*, *Sir* (and in Great Britain *Razzle*, *Men Only*, *Spick* and *Span*), and the aforementioned titles that the now-ambitious Norma Jeane was increasingly featured in.

In many cases, the "seedy" reputation of such titles was not entirely unwarranted. In those innocent but puritanical times, many so-called glamour publications exuded the prurience of the strip club and burlesque stage. Marilyn, on the other hand, brought to pinup photography a freshness and a guilt-free honesty that shone through from the start. And the photographer who captured this quality most vibrantly in a series of now-historic sessions was a young Hungarian war refugee called Andrés de Dienes.

Already with something of a reputation as a fashion photographer in New York, Dienes arrived in Los Angeles in late 1945 looking for a model to take on an idyllic photo-shoot trip in various beach, desert, and mountain locations. The Blue Book Modeling Agency suggested Norma Jeane, and when he met her Dienes was immediately smitten, and hired her for $100 a week plus expenses and props.

…it was as if a miracle had happened to me. Norma Jeane seemed to be like an angel. I could hardly believe it for a few moments.

**Andrés de Dienes**

Aunt Ana gave the expedition her blessing, assuring Dienes that the marriage to Jim Dougherty was all but over by this time, and, although she never posed nude on the trip, Norma Jeane and the enamoured photographer did become lovers.

Dienes' photographs subsequently appeared in a variety of magazines over the coming months, and indeed for the next couple of years. Any thoughts of marriage he had, however, were undermined as soon as they got back to Los Angeles, where Norma Jeane began working with other, more famous Hollywood photographers, including Richard C. Miller, Earl Moran, and Bruno Bernard. It became clear that she was putting her blossoming career before both her current husband and any other relationships in the near future.

It was a career she now had mapped out in her mind as culminating on the cinema screen rather than the front pages of pinup magazines. But it was via such a magazine, from a photo shoot with the renowned glamour photographer Bruno Bernard—known professionally as "Bernard of Hollywood"—that her first real encounter with the movie industry came about. He allegedly met Norma Jeane on the street in September 1945, arranging a sitting with her. Photo sessions that followed included a picture (as Jean Norman) that appeared on the cover of *Laff* pinup magazine—this, helped by some hustling from the redoubtable Emmeline Snively, coming to the attention of 20th Century Fox talent scout and casting director, Ben Lyon.

And the magazine shoots didn't stop as Hollywood beckoned; far from it, they proliferated all the more as Ben Lyon's newly named Marilyn Monroe began to get noticed, in a few short years becoming the most celebrated pinup girl of all time.

*Below and right:* **Pinup calendars, 1946**

Right, Norma Jeane poses for a portrait entitled "Bus Stop" by the artist and photographer, Earl Moran. Moran hired her as a model from February 1946, paying her ten dollars an hour to pose for photographs from which he painted, or sketched in charcoal and chalk, sexy "pinup" portraits for calendars such as the one below. "She liked to pose," Moran said later. "For her it was acting, and emotionally she did everything right."

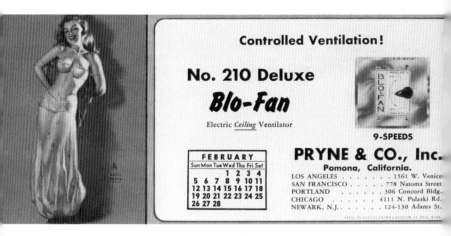

She was a clean-cut, American, wholesome girl—too plump, but beautiful in a way. We tried to teach her how to pose, how to handle her body. She always tried to lower her smile because she smiled too high, and it made her nose look a little long. At first she knew nothing about carriage, posture, walking sitting, or posing.

**Emmeline**

*Left:* **Zuma Beach, March 1946**

Joseph Jasgur, a celebrity photographer whose work had appeared in magazines such as *Silver Screen* and *Photoplay*, did some test shots of Norma Jeane for Emmeline Snively's Blue Modeling Book Agency. His first impression was of "a shy girl, nothing like a typical model, all breathless and anxious." But Jasgur was captivated by his new model's style, and had further sessions with her. Here they prepare for a shoot on a windswept Zuma Beach.

*Above:* **Family Circle, April 26, 1946**

*Right:* **Andrés de Dienes original, late 1945**
The first time Marilyn Monroe—as Norma Jeane Baker, of course—made an appearance on the front cover of a national magazine was this edition of *Family Circle*, taken at one of her earliest sessions with Andrés de Dienes.

The impact Norma Jeane had on me was tremendous.
As minutes passed, I fell more and more in love with
Norma Jeane.

**Andrés de Dienes**

*Above and left:* **Death Valley, California, December 1945**

Two years after it was taken, one of Andrés de Dienes' pictures of Norma Jeane in Death Valley appeared on the cover of the UK weekly *Picture Post*. The road trip in the winter of 1945 was something of a photographic odyssey, with Dienes recalling years later: "I bought Norma Jeane various clothes to wear for my pictures and keep her warm because it was December and my plans were to visit the desert, the mountains, everywhere in California, Nevada, Arizona, anywhere my fancy would dictate going."

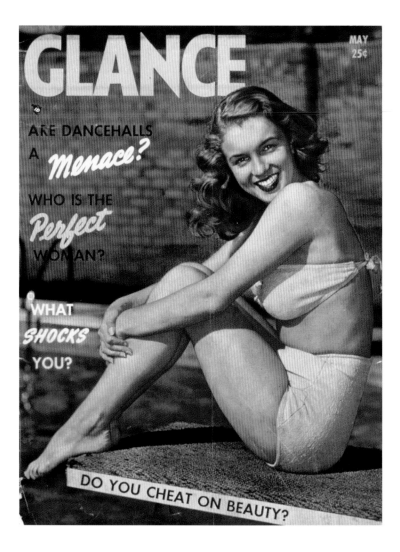

GLANCE

MAY
25¢

ARE DANCEHALLS A *Menace?*

WHO IS THE *Perfect* WOMAN?

WHAT *SHOCKS* YOU?

DO YOU CHEAT ON BEAUTY?

*Above:* **Bernard of Hollywood portrait, 1946**

The movie capital's leading glamour photographer, Bruno Bernard, known professionally as "Bernard of Hollywood," took many pictures of Norma Jeane (and later Marilyn) through the late 1940s and early 1950s.

*Left:* **Glance magazine, May 1949**

Bernard's pictures often ended up on the covers of men's magazines such as *Glance*. He once advised Norma Jeane, "Blend waif with Venus, and you'll create combustion in photos."

*Right:* **Photographs by Bill Burnside, 1946**

Another photographer who discovered Marilyn via Emmeline Snively's agency was the Scotsman William Burnside, who embarked on a brief affair with Norma Jeane, years later recalling the "lost look in the middle of a smile" that had attracted him. Ms Snively, on the other hand, viewed her protégé's success in a more professional light: "She started out with less than any girl I ever knew, but she worked the hardest … she wanted to learn, wanted to be somebody, more than anybody I saw before in my life."

## chapter 2

# Glamour girl, Hollywood hopeful

# "She radiated sex" 1946–52

With the encouragement of photographers including David Conover, Andrés de Dienes and Earl Moran—not to mention Grace Goddard—Norma Jeane mentioned to Emmeline Snively the possibilities of the movie business. Like most aspiring "models" around Los Angeles, a career in the Hollywood film studios was the ultimate goal, and Snively was the first to agree. There were plenty of opportunities for attractive young women, and to this end most of the big studios had their "stables" of starlets, although many of the hopefuls were never to get much further than small non-speaking walk-on parts.

To facilitate this, Snively initiated a temporary name change to Jean Norman—with which Norma Jeane wasn't particularly happy—and a change of hair style from a curly "dirty blonde" (as she called it) to a wavy golden blonde. At the same time, Norma Jeane moved in to a room at the Studio Club, an establishment run by Hollywood executives' wives for young women just starting (or struggling to get a start) in the movie business.

After hooking up with a powerful talent agency, the National Concert Artists Corporation, Norma Jeane found herself in the office of the head of new talent at 20th Century Fox, Ben Lyon, in July 1946. Asking her to read a few lines from the script of a 1944 wartime drama, *Winged Victory*, Lyon was clearly as impressed by her appearance as by her reading.

Two days later, a screen test was arranged with director Walter Lang who was shooting a new Betty Grable film at the time. Lyon asked him to shoot 100 feet of silent color film of Norma Jeane, with the famous cinema photographer, Leon Shamroy. After being made up, and dressed in a full-length gown, she was directed to walk across the floor, sit on a high stool, light a cigarette, stub it out and walk to a window at the side of the set. This was a purely visual test with no dialogue and no soundtrack. As she did when in front of the magazine photographers, as soon as Lang shouted "Action!" and the camera started whirring, the previously nervous Norma Jeane suddenly exuded a confident, almost unconscious, sex appeal.

After showing the test to studio supremo Daryl F. Zanuck, Ben Lyon offered Norma Jeane Dougherty a six-month contract, paying her a guaranteed $75 a week whether she worked or not, with an option for the studio to renew it for a further six months at an increased wage. Apparently, when Lyon gave her the news of the offer, she broke down in tears.

A few days before the contract was finalized, on August 24, Norma Jeane was summoned to Ben Lyon's office again; the matter of her name had to be settled once and for all. Neither party was happy with the "Jean Norman" that had appeared on some of her latest magazine shots, but Norma Jeane Dougherty was clearly out of the question. The surname itself was too cumbersome, but Norma Jeane immediately opted for her mother's family name, Monroe, and Lyon liked it. At the same time he recalled an actress of the 1920s who Norma Jeane reminded him of (and who he had been engaged to briefly), a blonde star of Broadway musicals called Marilyn Miller. Marilyn Monroe sounded perfect.

By the time her divorce was confirmed in September 1946, Norma Jeane—as Jim Dougherty was to recall later—had truly been succeeded by Marilyn Monroe. The new starlet, though getting no immediate work at the studio, spent her days introducing herself around the Fox lot learning all she could about costume, make-up, even lighting and other aspects which would impact on her

now-dedicated ambition in movies. At the same time, Helen Ainsworth at the National Concert Artists agency had appointed Harry Lipton as personal agent to Marilyn, and his efforts, plus those of the studio's own high-powered publicity department made sure her name (and picture) was being seen in more and more gossip columns and movie magazines.

The studio also sent Marilyn to informal classes held by the Actors Laboratory on nearby Crescent Heights Boulevard. This was a group of writers, actors, and directors from New York who staged workshops and plays with a "serious" content, and whose personnel included Phoebe Brand, with whom Marilyn studied in an ad hoc fashion through 1947. This was her first encounter with the group belonging to what would later be dubbed the "Method school"—people such as Elia Kazan and Lee Strasberg who were to be highly influential in her future acting career.

Meanwhile, at the beginning of that year, Fox renewed her contract for a further six months and gave Marilyn her first role in a movie—a walk-on part in a light comedy called *Scudda-Hoo! Scudda-Hey!* Most of the already brief scenes she shot were edited out of the final version of the movie, which starred June Haver and an eight-year-old Natalie Wood, but, crucially, Marilyn Monroe was now up there on screen—a place where she most definitely intended to stay.

Next at Fox came three short appearances in a teen melodrama entitled *Dangerous Years*, which was shot in May 1947 and released in December, four months before her equally forgettable debut vehicle *Scudda-Hoo! Scudda-Hay!*

*Left:* **With Ben Lyon, 1955**
Marilyn at the height of her fame with the man who discovered her.

August 1947 saw a potentially traumatic let-down: the studio declined their option to renew her contract for a further period. After the initial shock, Marilyn—ever growing in confidence—seemed to take it in her stride. She spent the next few months of enforced unemployment acquainting herself even more thoroughly with both the highbrow world of the Actors Lab and the social milieu of the Hollywood movie community.

And it was through a burgeoning personal contact network—specifically, Fox cofounder Joe Schenck (with whom she had by this time had an affair) and his friend Columbia boss Harry Cohen—that the latter's studio signed her to a six-month contract in March 1948. By the summer she was cast in her third film, a B-movie musical, *Ladies of the Chorus*, but more importantly her short tenure at Columbia introduced her to the daunting woman who was to be her drama coach for the next six years, Natasha Lytess.

Lytess was a formidable German who had studied under the great director Max Reinhardt, before fleeing to America as a refugee before World War II. She ended up in Hollywood, as a drama coach first at MGM and then Columbia. Her stern manner both intimidated and impressed her pupils—delivered in a harsh Slavic-sounding accent that promised no mercy, or so it seemed. But, however unlikely, there evolved a unique chemistry between her and Marilyn.

A more considered view is that the dependence upon each other became mutual. Nevertheless, Lytess lobbied for her pupil when they were casting *Ladies of the Chorus* and, although another unmemorable piece of cinema, it did reveal the first hints of Marilyn Monroe's natural talent as an actress—and singer. If anything, she overacted an undemanding part—clearly Lytess's influence coming into play—but people began to take notice.

One who certainly took notice was studio musician and vocal

coach Fred Karger, with whom Marilyn embarked on a passionate affair. But by early 1949, her contract expired and not renewed at Columbia, she was once again unemployed until Groucho Marx gave her a small part in a Marx Brothers comedy, *Love Happy*. Marx said he was looking for "… a young lady who can walk by me in such a manner as to arouse my elderly libido and cause smoke to issue from my ears."

By the time the film premiered in 1950 Marilyn Monroe had enjoyed more favorable publicity, so much so that she was credited separately in the movie as "Introducing Marilyn Monroe."

Still featuring in a modeling role, albeit with a movie-actress link, in magazines, and still more or less penniless despite the intermittent film work, in May 1949 she took part in a nude photo shoot for photographer Tom Kelley. The appearance of the pictures in a calendar was to cause a scandal three years later, when she was on the brink of a much bigger period in her career.

Towards the end of 1949 Marilyn met Johnny Hyde, a powerful Hollywood talent scout who worked for the influential William Morris Agency. Thirty years her senior, he was besotted with her from the start, vowing that he would make her a star. He subsequently introduced her to the highest echelons of Hollywood society while tirelessly lobbying the industry on her behalf. He even proposed marriage, which Marilyn turned down.

For the next couple of years Marilyn played in a varied array of motion pictures, from more bottom-of-the-cast-list parts—as in the film after *Love Happy*, *Ticket To Tomahawk*—to her first starring role, along with Richard Widmark, in the 1952 noir thriller *Don't Bother To Knock*. Between those releases, the most significant jobs she got were two 1950 movies made by her most prestigious directors yet: the John Huston thriller *The Asphalt Jungle*, followed by the satire

*All About Eve* directed by Joseph L. Mankiewicz and starring Bette Davis. These were the two films, both with minor speaking roles, that enabled her—along with burgeoning "Hollywood glamour girl" publicity—to take the next step up the ladder to stardom.

At the end of 1950, Johnny Hyde's promise was made good when he negotiated a seven-year contract with her original employers 20th Century Fox, after the success the studio had with the Oscar-nominated *All About Eve*. Hyde himself died just a week later. It was also at this time that Marilyn met two people who were to have a significant impact on her later professional and personal life, the director Elia Kazan and the Pulitzer prize-winning playwright, Arthur Miller.

Under the Fox contract, Marilyn was still "leased out" to other studios for certain films, the only one of significance after *Asphalt Jungle* and *All About Eve* being *Clash By Night*, directed by the veteran German filmmaker Fritz Lang; the only one, that is, until she landed her first lead part with British director Roy Ward Baker in *Don't Bother To Knock* in 1952.

It was a frantic time in her career. The fall of 1951 had seen her first full-length feature in a major magazine, *Colliers*, followed by cover stories in both *Look* and *Life*. Production of *Don't Bother To Knock* almost came to a standstill when the "scandal" of the 1949 nude calendar shoot broke in the media, now anxious for any titbits of gossip about the "blonde bombshell." Then, in June 1952, Fox announced she had a starring role in what would be one of their biggest movies of 1953, as Lorelei Lee in *Gentlemen Prefer Blondes*. Before that, however, she was going to take the movie-going public—and critics—by storm, in a melodrama that began shooting that same June, *Niagara*.

This girl had something I hadn't seen since silent pictures. She had a kind of fantastic beauty like Gloria Swanson and she radiated sex like Jean Harlow. She didn't need a soundtrack to tell her story.

**Leon Shamroy, cameraman**

# I'm going to be a great movie star some day.

*Left and previous page:* **Pictures by Bernard of Hollywood, 1946**
Among Marilyn's many sessions with Bernard, the one on the left—via a
cover shot for *Laff* magazine—first drew the attention of 20th Century Fox.

*Next page:* **First screen test, July 19, 1946**
Marilyn, in full-length crinoline gown, on her first screen test at Fox, which
was with director Walter Lang and the famed cameraman Leon Shamroy.

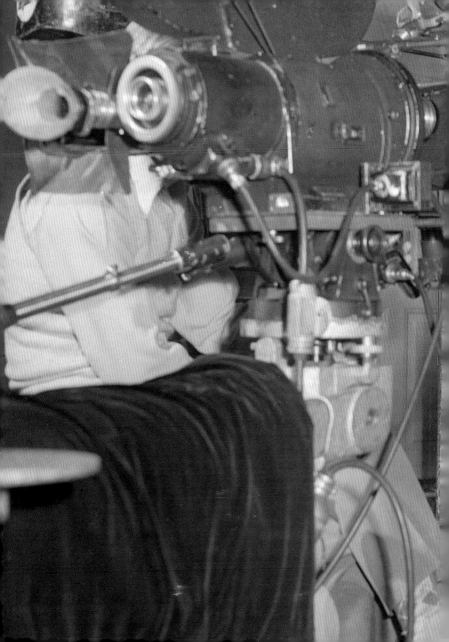

*Left:* **"Baby-sitting," June 1947**

The publicity department at Fox were never short of ideas when trying to promote up-and-coming new starlets. One they cooked up for Marilyn (complete with photos!) was her being "discovered" after baby-sitting for a studio executive.

**(Fox) Publicity made up a story about how I was a baby-sitter for a casting director ... you think they would have at least made me a daddy-sitter.**

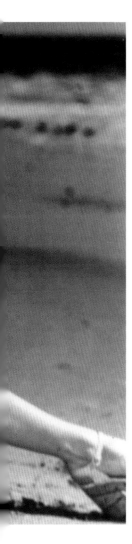

## Sex is part of nature.
## I go along with nature.

*Left and above:* **Beach shoot, 1947/Scope, 1951**
Photos from Marilyn's pinup shoots were used over
and over, as on this *Scope* cover four years later.

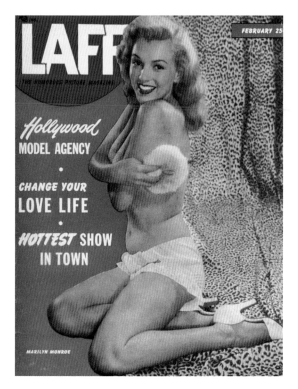

*Above and right:* **Pinup pictures, 1947**

Marilyn's modeling career was boosted in no uncertain terms by her debut in movies, even though her profile was still decidedly low. But, as Emmeline Snively of the Blue Book Modeling Agency was quick to point out, it wasn't just a matter of good looks and good fortune:

"Girls ask me all the time how they can be like Marilyn Monroe. And I tell them, if they showed one tenth of the hard work and gumption that that girl had, they'd be on their way. But there will never be another like her."

*Left:* **Warrenburg, NY, 1949**

As a budding star, Marilyn made plenty of "guest appearances" such as this one, presenting the prize to the winner of *Photoplay* magazine's "Dream House" contest in 1949.

*Above and right:* **Tobey Beach, Long Island, 1949**

In 1949 Marilyn took part in a promotional tour for the film *Love Happy* which took her through various major cities across the country, including New York. Also living on the East Coast at the time was the photographer with whom she had embarked on her memorable "road trip" back in 1945, Andrés de Dienes, and a shoot was organized out on Tobey Beach, Long Island, which produced some of the most stunning pictures of Marilyn ever taken. Four years later a shot appeared on the cover of *Modern Man* shown above, which featured an "I Knew Her When..." piece by Dienes.

... she could barely speak a word freely. Her habit of barely moving her lips when she spoke was unnatural ... All this I tried to teach Marilyn. But she knew her sex appeal was infallible, that it was the one thing on which she could depend.

**Natasha Lytess, drama coach**

*Left:* **Valentine, c. 1950**
Much of the modeling any aspiring movie actress undertook had to have a gimmick, such as the "cowgirl" pose seen here, no doubt destined for the Valentine's Day edition of a movie fan magazine.

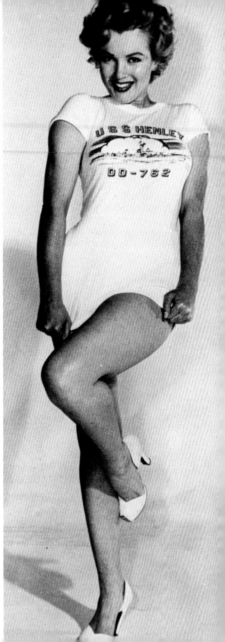

*Right:* **Publicity shot, c. 1951**
Marilyn always had a great
following in the armed forces.
Here she wears a T-shirt with a
USS *Hemley* logo.

*Far right:* **Korea, October 1952**
The forces connection made
good publicity, as with this shot
of Marines from the Devil Cats
Squadron in Korea, and their
collection of pinups that
included more than 200 shots
of Marilyn.

Over the years Hollywood has given us its "It Girl," its "Oomph Girl," its "Sweater Girl," and even "The Body." Now we get the "Mmmmmmm Girl."

**Earl Wilson, columnist**

*Right:* **"Potato sack" shots, c. 1952**

When a witty journalist commented that Marilyn would look good in a potato sack, the clever folk at the 20th Century Fox publicity office quickly asked photographer Earl Theisen to take some appropriate shots.

*Above and left:* **Cheesecake Queen, 1952**

Miss Cheesecake was an award given by *The Stars and Stripes*, the US Forces magazine, for their favorite pinup. Marilyn had won it in 1951, and in 1952, when this picture was taken, was made "Cheesecake Queen of 1952." Even before her movie career had taken off she had gained many such awards for her glamour—particularly from the armed forces—including the outrageously named "The Girl They Would Most Like to Intercept" award from the All Weather Fighter Squadron 3, San Diego. The term "cheesecake" was a slang expression at the time that referred to any good-looking pinup female, the male equivalent being dubbed "beefcake."

# ★ Scudda-Hoo! Scudda-Hay!

A lightweight "rural romance" in which Marilyn is seen just once in long-shot, paddling a canoe on a lake.

Studio: 20th Century Fox
Released: April 1948
Producer: Walter Morosco

Director: F. Hugh Herbert
Format: Technicolor
Leads: June Haver, Lon McCallister

Nobody discovered her, she earned her own way to stardom.

**Darryl F. Zanuck, president of 20th Century Fox**

##  Dangerous Years

Earnest drama addressing the subject of juvenile delinquency. Marilyn played Eve, a waitress, with three short scenes and some minimal dialogue.

Studio: 20th Century Fox
Released: December 1947
Producer: Sol W. Wurtzel

Director: Arthur Pierson
Format: Monochrome
Leads: William Halop, Ann E. Todd (née Mayfield)

 **Ladies of the Chorus**

A lightweight showbiz story in which Marilyn was able to act, dance, and even sing two songs—"Anyone Can Tell I Love You" and "Every Baby Needs a Da Da Daddy."

Studio: **Columbia**
Released: **October 1948**
Producer: **Harry A. Romm**

Director: **Phil Karlson**
Format: **Monochrome**
Leads: **Adele Jergens, Rand Brooks**

*Right:* **With Groucho Marx, 1950**

Talking about the casting of Marilyn in the movie, *Love Happy*, Marx said he was looking for "… a young lady who can walk by me in such a manner as to arouse my elderly libido and cause smoke to issue from my ears."

*Next page:* **Love Happy poster, date unknown**

A poster for *Love Happy,* designed some time after the film's original release, hence the claim that the movie "discovered" Marilyn Monroe.

 ★ **Love Happy**

In what is considered by many of their fans as the Marx Brothers' least accomplished movie, Marilyn plays a client of Groucho's detective, Sam Grunion.

Studio: **United Artists**
Released: **April 1950**
Producer: **Lester Cowan**

Director: **David Miller**
Format: **Monochrome**
Leads: **Harpo Marx, Chico Marx, Illona Massey**

The P
MA

ILONA MASSEY · VERA-ELLEN
MARION HUTTON

··· Raymond Burr·Melville Cooper·Leon Belasco·Paul Valentine·Eric Blore·Bruce Gordon
· MARY PICKFORD'S Presentation of A LESTER COWAN Production
Directed by DAVID MILLER·Musical Score & Lyrics by Ann Ronell
Released thru United Artists

The Picture That Discovered
MARILYN MONROE

LOVE HAPPY

starring

THE Marx Bros.

# The nude calendar sessions

In the spring of 1949, despite having just made a movie with the Marx Brothers, up-and-coming Hollywood actress Marilyn Monroe was broke—or, at least, always watching where the next dollar, the next paycheck, was coming from. So, between films, it was down to glamour model Marilyn to pay the rent when the chance arose.

This time it was the photographer, Tom Kelley, who came to the rescue. Marilyn had introduced herself to him and his wife Natalie, looking for photographic work, at the beginning of May. Kelley immediately sensed she had "something," and a couple of weeks later one of his pictures from the subsequent session was on a new poster for Pabst beer.

The beer ad was noticed by a Chicago calendar publisher, who contacted Kelley with a view to a nude photo of the same model. So it was that Kelley contacted Marilyn to negotiate what would turn out to be the most notorious modeling session of her career.

Not averse to the idea of nudity—and she had done plenty of partially-nude work by this time—Marilyn accepted the $50 she urgently needed to settle an overdue payment on her secondhand convertible car. On May 27 she arrived at the photographic studio where Kelley and Natalie greeted her, made her at ease, and commenced to photograph her lying unclothed on a red velvet drape they had laid out on the floor, Kelley poised ten feet above her on a ladder.

Compared to previous nude photography—which was, in the main, province of a few pre-*Playboy* girlie books if not out-and-out pornography—the dozens of shots constituted a refreshingly honest celebration of the human female form, devoid of sleaze or prurience. Just a handful of them survive.

Kelley remembers Marilyn as a hard worker, not possessing the "difficult" attitude that was to plague numerous photographers in later years—some of whom complained of having to wait hour after hour for her to prepare her make-up.

It was three years later, while Marilyn was making *Don't Bother To Knock* that the "scandal" surrounding the calendar broke. Handled the wrong way, or allowed to be blown out of proportion by the gossip columns and "yellow journalism" tabloid magazines, it could have ruined her career. But, despite the studio's immediate instinct to bury the story with shocked denials from the rising star, Marilyn readily admitted that it was she who had posed for Kelley's camera when she was confronted by United Press International (UPI) Hollywood correspondent Aline Mosby; she pleaded poverty as mitigating circumstance with a wide-eyed innocence that was almost universally endearing. Consequently one of the shots— dubbed "Golden Dreams"—appeared as the centerfold in the first edition of *Playboy* magazine, published in December 1953. For years thereafter, she would autograph copies of the calendar for servicemen with consummate pride.

I felt shy about it, but they were real delicate ... about the whole situation. They just spread out some red velvet and had me lie down on it. And it was all very simple—and drafty!

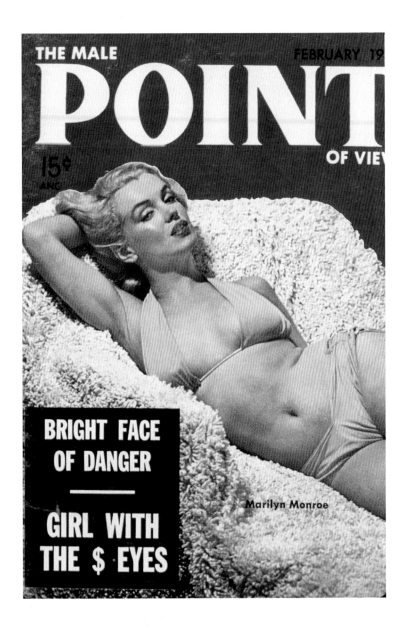

THE MALE

FEBRUARY 19

# POINT

OF VIEW

15¢
ANC

BRIGHT FACE
OF DANGER
———
GIRL WITH
THE $ EYES

Marilyn Monroe

# You could not photograph her badly if you tried.

**Inge Morath, photographer**

*Left:* **Pin-up picture, early 1950s**
The nude session notwithstanding, Marilyn continued to pursue her work as a pin-up model in parallel with her burgeoning film career, the one activity promoting the other. By the early Fifties she had appeared on literally hundreds of magazine covers, the number increasing as her film career took off.

# It's all make-believe, isn't it?

## ★ A Ticket to Tomahawk

Marilyn plays chorus girl Clara in this spoof Western, in which she sings one song with Dan Dailey, "Oh, What A Forward Young Man."

Studio: 20th Century Fox
Released: May 1950
Producer: Robert Bassler

Director: Richard Sale
Format: Technicolor
Leads: Dan Dailey, Ann Baxter,
Rory Calhoun

## ⭐ The Asphalt Jungle

A tough thriller about the executing and aftermath of a robbery, in which Marilyn was cast as Angela Phinlay, girlfriend of crooked lawyer, played by Louis Calhern.

Studio: Metro-Goldwyn-Mayer

Released: May 1950

Producer: Arthur Hornblower

Director: John Huston

Format: Monochrome

Leads: Sterling Hayden, Louis Calhern

Marilyn was one step from oblivion when I directed her in The Asphalt Jungle. I remember she impressed me more off the screen than on ... there was something touching and appealing about her.

**John Huston**

*Previous page:* **Publicity shot, The Asphalt Jungle, 1950**
Director John Huston said of Marilyn's screen test for the role in *The Asphalt Jungle:* "When it was over, Marilyn looked very insecure about the whole thing and asked to do it over. I agreed. But I had already decided on the first take. The part of Angela was hers."

*Above:* **The Asphalt Jungle, 1950**
Marilyn as Angela, the lawyer's "moll," in the arms of her older lover—
played by Louis Calhern, a veteran of Hollywood movies since the days of
silent films.

*Left:* **Publicity photo, All About Eve, 1950**

A publicity portrait with Marilyn wearing her dress from the movie, designed by the Oscar-winning Hollywood costumer, Edith Head.

 **All About Eve**

A sophisticated social satire, with Marilyn's portrayal of Miss Caswell—though eighth down on the cast list—attracting the most attention she had yet enjoyed.

Studio: **20th Century Fox**
Released: **October 1950**
Producer: **Darryl F. Zanuck**

Director: **Joseph L. Mankiewicz**
Format: **Monochrome**
Leads: **Bette Davis, Anne Baxter, George Sanders**

*Right:* **The Fireball, 1950**
Marilyn's "Polly" cheers on the roller stars, with James Brown (center) and Mickey Rooney.

 **The Fireball**

Justifiably badly received "comedy" in which Marilyn had a minor part as a roller-derby groupie.

**Studio:** Metro-Goldwyn-Mayer
**Released:** November 1950
**Producer:** Bert E. Friedlob

**Director:** Tay Garnett
**Format:** Monochrome
**Leads:** Mickey Rooney, Pat O'Brien

> **[Hollywood is] a place where they'll pay you a thousand dollars for a kiss and fifty cents for your soul.**

If you're good, I'll tell you the recipe.
I know the ingredients.

Dick Powell inviting Marilyn to a home-made dinner in her
brief appearance in Right Cross

 **Right Cross**

Boxing romance—Marilyn's brief appearance as Dusky Le Doux in a club
scene not even making the cast list.

Studio: Metro-Goldwyn-Mayer

Released: November 1950

Producer: Armand Deutsch

Director: John Sturges

Format: Monochrome

Leads: June Allyson, Dick Powell

# ★ Home Town Story

A strange one-hour film financed by American industry as a propaganda vehicle for corporate business in which Marilyn plays Iris, an office receptionist plagued by the unwelcome attention of her boss.

**Studio:** Metro-Goldwyn-Mayer
**Released:** May 1951
**Producer:** Arthur Pierson

**Director:** Arthur Pierson
**Format:** Monochrome
**Leads:** Jeffrey Lynn, Donald Crisp

*Right:* **As Young As You Feel, 1951**

Marilyn poses with her name not quite up there in lights, but certainly on the billboard.

## ★ As Young As You Feel

Romantic comedy, with Marilyn again playing a company boss's secretary, Harriet. The *New York Times'* critic described her performance as "superb."

**Studio:** 20th Century Fox
**Released:** August 1951
**Producer:** Lamar Trotti

**Director:** Harmon Jones
**Format:** Monochrome
**Leads:** Monty Woolley, Jean Peters, Thelma Ritter

WMAN-A-635
ARILYN MONROE
"AS ROBERTA"
1 # 8
INT. APT. DOORWAY
SC 133

4/12/51 DES-RENIE

*Above:* **Shoe advertisement, 1951**

Indicative of Marilyn's growing appeal to the male market was this unlikely use of her name and face to advertise men's shoes!

 **Love Nest**

Lundigan's old army buddy "Bobby" turns out to be recently discharged WAC Roberta—played by Marilyn, third on the cast list—who moves in with him and his less-than-pleased wife.

Studio: **20th Century Fox**
Released: **October 1951**
Producer: **Jules Buck**

Director: **Joseph M. Newman**
Format: **Monochrome**
Leads: **William Lundigan, June Haver**

# ★ Let's Make It Legal

A farce, highly forgettable but for the presence of Marilyn as the sexy fortune-hunter Joyce eyeing Zachary Scott and his millions.

Studio: 20th Century Fox
Released: November 1951
Producer: Robert Bassler

Director: Richard Sale
Format: Monochrome
Leads: Claudette Colbert, Macdonald Carey, Zachary Scott

You can't sleep your way into being a star ... it takes much, much more. But it helps. A lot of actresses got their first chance that way. Most of the men are such horrors, they deserve all they can get out of them!

*Left:* **Let's Make It Legal, 1951**

Marilyn in a bathing-suit scene from *Let's Make It Legal*, which its publicity described as "10% illegal ... 40% improper ... 100% hilarious!"

*Next pages:* **Life magazine, April 7, 1952**

Photographer Philippe Halsman took one of the earliest truly iconic images of Marilyn for an article in *Life* magazine entitled "Marilyn Monroe: The Talk of Hollywood." Describing the shoot—for which we can also see her preparing in the pictures on the right—Halsman recalled "I was facing her with my camera, the *Life* reporter and assistant at my side. Marilyn was cornered and she flirted with all three of us, and the photograph eventually made the cover of *Life*. The cover gave her the status of a star..."

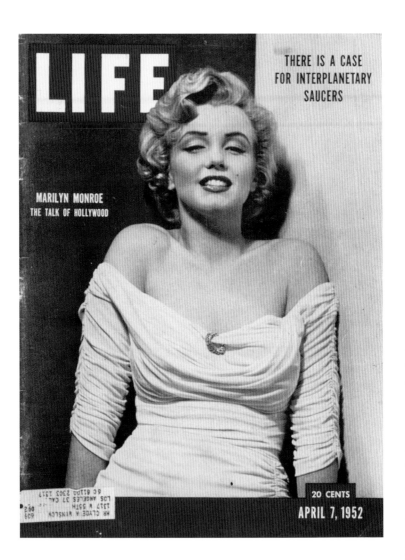

**LIFE**

THERE IS A CASE
FOR INTERPLANETARY
SAUCERS

MARILYN MONROE
THE TALK OF HOLLYWOOD

20 CENTS

APRIL 7, 1952

112

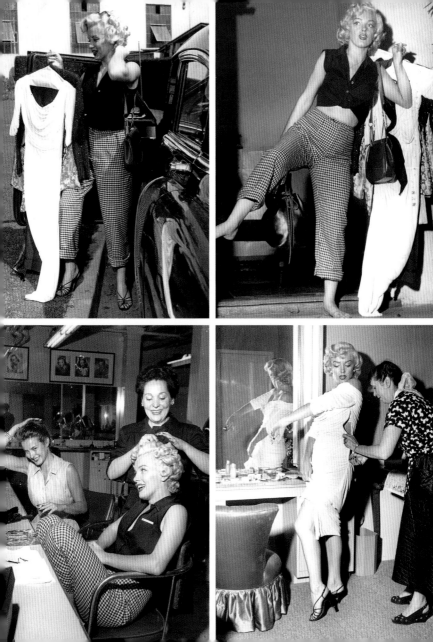

*Right:* **Clash By Night, 1952**
Marilyn in another bathing-suit scene, this time from *Clash By Night*. The movie's co-producer Jerry Wald was to later comment, "Marilyn Monroe is the greatest farceuse in the business, a female Chaplin."

**She was a very peculiar mixture of shyness and uncertainty and—I wouldn't say "star allure"—but she knew exactly her impact on men.**

**Fritz Lang, director**

## ★ Clash By Night

A tense drama in which Marilyn, as cannery worker Peggy, was in danger of being eclipsed by the heavyweight leads but garnered some good notices from the critics.

Studio: RKO Radio Pictures
Released: June 1952
Producer: Harriet Parsons, a Jerry Wald-Norman Krssna Production

Director: Fritz Lang
Format: Monochrome
Leads: Barbara Stanwyck, Paul Douglas, Robert Ryan

They *called it love!*

But that isn't what the whole town whispered...nor the ugly name the husband gave it when he found out ...too late!

# NIGHT

d by FRITZ LANG • Screenplay by ALFRED HAYES

3

# ★ We're Not Married

A star-studded anthology comedy in which Marilyn's five-minute part was tailor-made as a "Miss Mississippi" beauty queen.

**Studio:** 20th Century Fox
**Released:** July 1952
**Producer:** Nunnally Johnson

**Director:** Edmund Goulding
**Format:** Monochrome
**Leads:** Victor Moore, Jane Darwell, Ginger Rogers, Marilyn Monroe, Paul Douglas, Mitzi Gaynor, Louis Calhern, Zsa Zsa Gabor

*Right:* **We're Not Married, 1952**
Marilyn in her brief role as Annabel Norris, winner of the "Miss Mississippi" beauty contest.

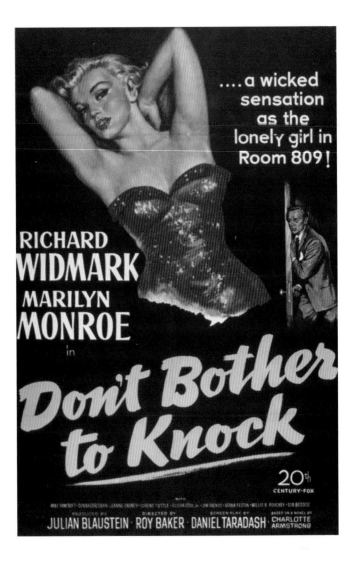

 **Don't Bother To Knock**

Tense noir-style thriller with Marilyn in her first lead part as the psychotic baby-sitter, Nell Forbes.

Studio: **20th Century Fox**
Released: **July 1952**
Producer: **Julian Baustein**

Director: **Roy Baker**
Format: **Monochrome**
Leads: **Richard Widmark, Marilyn Monroe, Anne Bancroft**

## When we looked at the rushes, she had the rest of us knocked off the screen!

### Richard Widmark

*Next page:* **Don't Bother To Knock, 1952**
Marilyn prepares for a promotional photo-call.

# Interview with Roy Ward Baker

**DIRECTOR, *DON'T BOTHER TO KNOCK***

London, January 21, 2004

Director Roy Ward Baker had cut his teeth in London studios during the 1930s as an assistant to Alfred Hitchcock and Carol Reed, progressing to making his own features after World War II, including the highly acclaimed war drama *Morning Departure*. In 1951 he directed *I'll Never Forget You* (titled *The House On The Square* in the UK), which, though made in England, was produced by Sol C. Siegel for 20th Century Fox.

His next assignment was to be made in Hollywood, a movie about a psychotic baby-sitter for which Marilyn Monroe had been earmarked to play the lead. From the start, the general opinion in the studio was that she had got the job via the powerful Fox executive Joe Schenck, with whom she was having, or had recently had, an affair. Whatever the truth of the matter may have been, the choice was queried by producer Julian Blaustein, Baker himself, and even studio boss (and Schenk partner) Zanuck. Zanuck—who never particularly liked Marilyn— felt that if they were going to make it with her, they would make it on the cheap.

"... I met the producer and we talked, he showed me the script and I read it, and so that was the idea, we should make it, but right from the start we both said to ourselves—and he possibly said it to Zanuck—we both said Marilyn Monroe is not right for this part. It's really for Jane Wyman, or if there's another Jane Wyman a bit younger, better still, but it was absolutely mandatory that Marilyn Monroe was going to play that part ... so of course in the end we accepted it, we had to.

"So we were tucked away in the Western Avenue studio, not in the main studio on Peco. I didn't mind, the Western Avenue studio was rather glamorous really because that was the original Hollywood. The producer was Julian Blaustein, and he had a sidekick called William Bloom who did most of the work. They were very nice fellows, both of them, very nice men. They were very good to me...

"So I embarked on this little saga completely innocent. At that time Marilyn was Joe Schenck's mistress. Schenck was the real boss of the studio, the senior partner with Zanuck. There again Zanuck was in charge of production, and they left him severely alone. So as I put it together afterward, it was Schenck who really fostered the idea of presenting this cast. One thing was clear to me at the time—I wasn't *totally* innocent—I went into the history of Marilyn's adventures up to that time, and she'd actually acted in fifteen pictures. She'd been around, so in many ways it was the last chance saloon for her."

**Baker, billed at that time simply as Roy Baker—recalls his first meeting with Marilyn in his 2000 memoir *A Director's Cut*.**

"I think the first time I met Marilyn was when we were discussing costuming with the designer, William Travilla, who became devoted to her and dressed her in almost all her films. At any rate, I do remember that she had two fat books under her arm, by Stanislavsky. We made her look as plain as possible at the beginning of the story, with little make-up and wearing an ill-fitting cotton dress—all of which made her look, if anything, more attractive. Then when she appeared in the later scenes in full make-up and a coffee-colored negligee she looked like the dazzling star she was destined to be.

*Left:* **A still from the movie, with her co-star, Richard Widmark.**

"So she was very overwrought and very nervous, and frightened to death and all that, the usual thing, and it was a very difficult job. I think I got her confidence in the end but it was a struggle and she did her best and I did my best and that was that.

"She was bedeviled by her coach who was a ... well, she was not the right person. She was of Russian-Polish-German background, Natasha Lytess. She bored on about Stanislavsky and all that stuff long before the Method got going—not too long but a few years, two or three years before that started to flourish—but she had Marilyn absolutely under her spell, and Marilyn couldn't move or breath without her. She was on the set all the time, until eventually I banned her from the set. I didn't realize you could do that, at least you could in those days, and Marilyn was very upset—but she took it, there was nothing she could do about it. I said 'Believe me, it's for your own good. You can't listen to two people, and everything's going fine, all going quietly along, but it's a struggle to do it when you're trying to do two different things at once'."

**When rehearsals started on December 7, 1951, Marilyn had already requested permission from Zanuck himself to allow Lytess on the set during shooting. The mogul's reply, quoted in full in Rudy Behlmer's *Memo from Daryl F. Zanuck* (1993), supported Baker's attitude, concluding:**

*"I think you are capable of playing this role without the help of anyone but the director and yourself. You have built up a Svengali and if you are going to progress with your career and become as important talent-wise as you have publicity-wise then you must destroy this Svengali before it destroys you. When I cast you for this role I cast you as an individual."*

"I mean Marilyn was not obstreperous or difficult like some of them can be, the prima donnas ... she was not a prima donna at all, far from it, and she had her own interests at heart. Underneath it all, it never really emerged anytime until much later on, she was really ruthlessly ambitious, but she had no intellect at all, she was anything but intellectual. But that was a bit of good luck as far as she was concerned, she didn't need it. She just had to be there and that was it. That really was the basis that I arrived at after about a week, that I'm not directing an actress, I'm directing a film star.

"And in a way I can prove it. There was a man called Dick Richards, he was the film and theater critic for the *Daily Mirror* no less, the London *Daily Mirror*. He arrived in Hollywood while I was in the middle of shooting this picture, so I said 'Come out to the studio, I want to show you something.' He duly arrived one afternoon and I gave him a cup of tea or whatever, and then I said 'Now I want you to meet this girl, because she is going to be an absolutely tip-top international star.' And so Marilyn was duly presented, and they chatted, and everything was fine, and he didn't believe me. He went home and he didn't do anything about it at all. Of course he dined out on the story ever since. I gave him a scoop.

"So that was really the basis that I found to deal with that situation with that particular girl. The other actors were marvelous, I mean they were bored witless by her continually fluffing and missing the moves and making a bosh-up, and 'Let's do it again, once more darling...' you know. It tired them out, they weren't at all at ease."

**After the film was finished, Baker left for Africa on another assignment. Returning to Hollywood he found *Don't Bother To Knock* had exceeded all expectations at the box office, undoubtedly because of Marilyn's increasingly high profile in the media.**

"When I got back I discovered that *Don't Bother To Knock* had been a roaring success, it absolutely ran away at the box office. Well you see, it couldn't help making money simply because Zanuck so disliked the whole idea of making it that he decided that if it's got to be made, then it's got to be made cheap. It was in profit in six weeks because it had been made for peanuts—it was probably the cheapest picture ever made at Fox! But there it was, and within a fortnight I was back busy again.

"And of course a very strange thing is, looking back, that this was 1952 and such a thing as a baby-sitter who turns out to be slightly, ever so slightly, psychopathic, was ludicrous. I mean … nanny was never like that! And so, in a way, the whole premise of the picture was on a very flimsy basis really, for those days. Thirty years later, fifty years later which it now is, we have psychopathic baby-sitters popping up all over the place!

"Hitch would have done a very good job on it, though there again, it wasn't until *Psycho* that he picked up on that psychiatric angle, before then it was straightforward adventures. I suppose to a certain extent I didn't want to push the drama too hard because it was on a slightly flimsy basis. If I'd really worked on it and made her obviously barmy, we could have gone over the top, for those days. Nowadays, you can go the full enchilada."

**Baker acknowledges that in a curious way, Marilyn's personal background and manner fitted the part very well.**

"Her background fitted, and I think she knew what she was talking about. I think that's why she—or whoever it was discovered this book—she probably thought 'That's for me.' "

# True
# Experiences

25 Complete Features For Only 25¢

The Magazine About Real People

May

Do I look happy?

I should—
For I was a child
nobody wanted
A lonely girl with a
dream—who awakened to find
that dream come true —

I am Marilyn Monroe....
read my Cinderella story on page 22 →

*Previous page:* **True Experiences, May 1952**

By the early summer of 1952, Marilyn Monroe was a famous enough name to make the front page of *True Experiences* magazine, announcing her "Cinderella Story" which was a "personal" account of her early life.

*Right:* **Monkey Business, 1952**

Running through her script with one of the cast of *Monkey Business*. The *New York Herald Tribune* wrote of the film: "Miss Monroe ... disproves more than adequately the efficacy of the old stage rule about not turning one's back to the audience."

## ★ Monkey Business

A comedy concerning a lab monkey that spills a youth potion into the water cooler, reducing all but the "dumb blonde" secretary to an infantile state.

Studio: **20th Century Fox**
Released: **September 1952**
Producer: **Sol C. Siegel**

Director: **Howard Hawks**
Format: **Monochrome**
Leads: **Cary Grant, Ginger Rogers**

She seemed very shy, and I remember that when the studio workers would whistle at her, it seemed to embarrass her.

**Cary Grant**

*Right:* **With Cary Grant in Monkey Business, 1952**
When the movie was released, Marilyn's name was on the up-and-up, so much so that cinemas ran her name above that of her more established co-stars, Cary Grant and Ginger Rogers.

# ★ O Henry's Full House

In this compendium movie of five separate stories, Marilyn was cast simply as "a streetwalker" in "The Cop and the Anthem."

Studio: 20th Century Fox
Released: October 1952
Producer: André Hakim

Director: Henry Koster
Format: Monochrome
Leads: (The Cop and the Anthem) Charles Laughton, Marilyn Monroe

Marilyn Monroe, again as sleek as she was in The Asphalt Jungle, is a streetwalker of stunning proportions.

**Archer Winston, New York Post**

*Left:* **Miss America, September 2, 1952**
When *Monkey Business* had its premier in Atlantic City, New Jersey, it was arranged for Marilyn to be the first female Grand Marshall of the Miss America Pageant, heading the parade in a revealing black number that drew a welter of publicity—via both photographers and protesting church groups—on account of its plunging neckline.

I am not interested in money.
I just want to be wonderful.

I knew I belonged to the public and to the world, not because I was talented or even beautiful, but because I had never belonged to anything or anyone else.

*Right:* **Cedars of Lebanon Hospital, April 1952**
Marilyn recovering in a Los Angeles hospital after having her appendix removed on April 28, 1952. The story goes that she was so terrified that the operation would harm her ability to have children, the surgeon found a note taped to her abdomen, asking him to cut as little as possible!

## chapter 3

# Pinup queen, movie star

# "Phenomenon of nature" 1952–54

Darryl F. Zanuck was impressed enough by Marilyn's performance in *Don't Bother To Knock* to cast her in another thriller, *Niagara*, within the year. This is despite not caring for her personally very much, and how "difficult," by virtue of her nervousness and what Roy Baker termed "stage fright," she had proved on the set.

A few months before the start of production in June 1952, Marilyn had started dating—seriously as it turned out—America's biggest baseball star of the era, Joe DiMaggio. From the start, he was protective of her, both from what he called the "phonies" and sycophants who were surrounding the rising star, and the leering eyes of the male population generally.

DiMaggio didn't like the fact that his girlfriend, who had appeared as a streetwalker in her last movie *O Henry's Full House*, was now being cast as a voluptuous young wife trying to murder her jealous husband. However, the film, shot largely on location at Niagara Falls, was a critical and box-office smash when released in 1953. Marilyn Monroe was well and truly on her way up to the top.

Marilyn's success in *Niagara* was followed by lead roles in the wildly popular *Gentlemen Prefer Blondes* and *How to Marry a Millionaire*. The much-heralded *Blondes* had her co-starring with one of Hollywood's well-established glamour queens, the buxom brunette Jane Russell. The publicity surrounding the movie's release was enormous, including the now-iconic shots of the two beauties kneeling together to leave their handprints outside Grauman's Chinese Theater on Hollywood Boulevard, as generations of stars had done before them. The film itself also established Marilyn as a movie vocalist with three songs, one of which she would be identified with forever after, "Diamonds Are A Girl's Best Friend."

*How To Marry a Millionaire* likewise teamed her with movie legends, this time the statuesque Lauren Bacall and 1940s pinup Betty Grable. *Photoplay* magazine voted Marilyn the Best New Actress of 1953, and at twenty-seven years old she was undeniably the best-loved blonde bombshell in Hollywood.

February 1954 saw Marilyn and Joe DiMaggio married, and, after a well-publicized honeymoon in Tokyo, Marilyn took time to perform for the service men stationed in Korea. Her presence caused a near-riot among the troops, and Joe was clearly uncomfortable with thousands of men ogling his new bride. Marilyn, on the other hand, was to remember it as one of the most fulfilling events of her career.

The marriage and publicity it garnered was enough to persuade Fox to drop a serious disciplinary matter in which she had been suspended in January 1954, after refusing to turn up for a new film, *The Girl In Pink Tights*. In it she was to play opposite Frank Sinatra, but learning he was to get $5,000 a week to her $1,500, this despite her being the bigger box-office draw, Marilyn made her protest by not showing up at the studio.

Next she was to hit the screens of the world opposite another Hollywood superstar, tough-guy actor Robert Mitchum. The film was an adventure set in the wilds of the West, *River Of No Return*, in which Marilyn again wowed the critics by her appearance, if not always her acting.

December 1954 saw the release of another full-color Cinemascope spectacular, the Irving Berlin musical *There's No Business Like Show Business*; it featured an all-star cast that included Ethel Merman, Dan Dailey, Donald O'Connor, Mitzi Gaynor and "cry-guy" singing heart-throb, Johnnie Ray. The glossy dance routines and lightweight character part served to confirm a stereotype casting that Marilyn was by now anxious to distance herself from, before it was too late.

Four months earlier, Marilyn had begun filming the motion picture which would represent the next important phase in her career, of a different order to the all-singing all-dancing razamatazz of *Show Business*. From a play by George Axelrod (who also wrote the screenplay), and directed by the great Billy Wilder, *The Seven Year Itch* was a sophisticated romantic comedy with Tom Ewell. It became as famous for its main publicity shot—of Marilyn standing over a New York subway grating with her skirt billowing up to her shoulders—as anything in the movie itself.

And it was that shot, and the attendant crowds who gathered in New York to see it take place, that was just too much for Joe DiMaggio. The couple had their worst marital tiff over it, leading to their separation in the October—Marilyn subsequently filing for divorce. They attributed the split to a "conflict of careers," and remained close friends thereafter. At the time of their break-up, Joe DiMaggio was the most famous sporting idol in America, but Marilyn Monroe was now the most famous screen idol in the world.

**That's the trouble, a sex symbol becomes a thing. But if I'm going to be a symbol of something, I'd rather have it sex than some other things we've got symbols of.**

WHY MEN FALL FOR GRACE KELLY

# Movieland

JUNE • 25 CENTS

A FAWCETT PUBLICATION

**SHOULD THESE MEN MARRY NOW?**

Clark Gable
Bing Crosby
Greg Peck
Marlon Brando
James Dean
Monty Clift

Marilyn Monroe

However admirably constructed Miss Monroe may be, she is hardly up to competing with one of the wonders of the continent.

**The New Yorker**

 Niagara

Thriller in which Marilyn is cast as Rose Loomis, adulterous wife of a jealous husband played by Joseph Cotten, whom she plans to murder while on vacation at Niagara Falls.

Studio: 20th Century Fox
Released: January 1953
Producer: Charles Brackett

Director: Henry Hathaway
Format: Technicolor
Leads: Marilyn Monroe, Joseph Cotten, Jean Peters

Marilyn Monroe and *Niagara*
a raging
torrent of
emotion
that even
nature can't
control!

20th CENTURY-FOX presents

# Niagara

TECHNICOLOR

STARRING

MARILYN MONROE · JOSEPH COTTEN · JEAN PETERS

WITH CASEY ADAMS · DENIS O'DEA · RICHARD ALLAN · DON WILSON · LURENE TUTTLE · RUSSELL COLLINS · WILL WRIGHT

PRODUCED BY CHARLES BRACKETT · DIRECTED BY HENRY HATHAWAY · WRITTEN BY CHARLES BRACKETT, WALTER REISCH AND RICHARD BREEN

Everything that girl does is sexy. A lot of people—the ones who haven't met Marilyn—will tell you it's all publicity. That's malarkey. They've tried to give a hundred other girls the same publicity build-up. It didn't take with them. This girl's really got it.

**Co-star Joseph Cotten**

*Left:* **Still from Niagara, 1952**
Marilyn in a charged shower scene with Joseph Cotten. The movie's director Henry Hathaway said later "I found her marvelous to work with and terrifically ambitious to do better. And bright. She may not have had an education, but she was just naturally bright."

150

*Left:* **Cosmetic advertisement, 1953**

Celebrity endorsement was always big business in Hollywood, and by the time *Niagara* was released Marilyn's name was clearly big enough to plug this line in cosmetics. Westmore, incidentally, was a legendary name in the movie capital, a family dynasty of make-up artists headed by father George —who began working with Rudolph Valentino in the 1920s—and six sons, all of whom worked for different studios right up to the 1970s.

## She can make any move, any gesture, almost unsufferably suggestive.

### Henry Hathaway, director

# Interview with Bob Willoughby
### PHOTOGRAPHER
Vence, France, February 11, 2004

**Photographer Bob Willoughby, renowned for his jazz photography, was sent to cover a publicity stunt set up by bandleader Ray Anthony and Fox. Trumpeter Anthony had released a single called "Marilyn" written by Ervin Drake and Jimmy Shirl, and held a launch party at his home. Marilyn was flown in by helicopter. In the media chaos that ensued she was photographed playing the drums under the direction of her co-star in 1950's The Fireball, Mickey Rooney.**

"Ray Anthony did a song called 'Marilyn.' She was flown in from Fox in a helicopter, and every photographer in Hollywood was there. I was working with Harpers at the time. What was I doing here I thought? My agent convinced me that everything about Marilyn Monroe was surefire news at that time, and I needed the work. She arrived in the chopper, and all the photographers rushed down to where she was getting out. Meanwhile the helicopter's backrush started blowing all the women's hats, papers, the band's sheet music, all into the swimming pool, it was chaotic. Then an incredible thing happened. Marilyn starts walking up the stairs right up to where I was standing on my own. I probably have the only pictures of Marilyn that day by herself. I guess someone was smiling down on me just then."

*Right:* **Los Angeles, 1952**
Trumpeter Ray Anthony and "drummer" Mickey Rooney pose either side of Marilyn, against a backdrop of the sheet music of the same name.

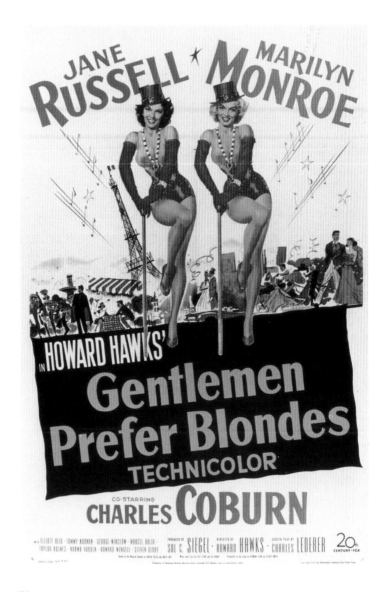

> There wasn't a real thing about her, everything was completely unreal.
>
> **Howard Hawks, director**

## ★ Gentlemen Prefer Blondes

Based on a book by Anita Loos, which then became a musical comedy. Marilyn plays gold-digger Lorelei Lee, a not-so-dumb blonde when it comes to weighing up men—and their bank balances.

Studio: 20th Century Fox
Released: July 1953
Producer: Sol C. Siegel

Director: Howard Hawks
Format: Technicolor
Leads: Jane Russell, Marilyn Monroe

Marilyn is a dreamy girl. She's liable to show up with one red shoe and one black shoe … I'd find out when we'd take a break at eleven that she hadn't had any breakfast and forgot she was hungry until I reminded her.

**Co-star Jane Russell**

*Right:* **Hollywood Boulevard, Los Angeles, June 26, 1953**
Wearing similar white polka-dot dresses, Marilyn and brunette bombshell Jane Russell put their hand-prints in the cement outside Grauman's Chinese Theater, a Hollywood tradition since the days of the silent movies.

*Next page:* **On set with Natasha Lytess, November 1952**
On the set of *Gentlemen Prefer Blondes*, an anxious-looking Marilyn takes some advice from her drama coach.

# The man who dressed Marilyn

The majority of Marilyn Monroe's costumes during her period as a leading lady and star were created by the Hollywood costume designer, Billy Travilla. Born in 1920, William Travilla—who was known professionally simply as "Travilla"—had his greatest recognition prior to working with Marilyn when he won an Oscar for the costumes in an Errol Flynn swashbuckling spectacular, *The Adventures of Don Juan,* in 1948.

He first met Marilyn in 1950 while one of several contract designers at 20th Century Fox, when she asked if she could borrow his fitting room in order to try on a costume. He was to work with her for the first time on *Monkey Business* in 1952. It was with *Gentlemen Prefer Blondes* the following year, however, that he established himself as Marilyn's "trademark" costume designer, creating not just the spectacular outfits in that movie but similarly iconic numbers for *How to Marry a Millionaire*, *River of No Return*, *There's No Business Like Show Business*, *The Seven Year Itch* and *Bus Stop*.

One such garment that appeared in *Gentlemen Prefer Blondes*, albeit briefly as it was deemed too revealing to pass the censors, was the body-hugging sheer gold lamé dress that Marilyn later wore for a ceremony at the Beverly Hills Hotel honoring her as "Fastest Rising Star" at the 1953 *Photoplay* awards. Travilla had to sew her into the floor-length gown with its plunging neckline, so tight was the fit. Not surprisingly, it caused a sensation.

*Right:* **Publicity shot, Gentlemen Prefer Blondes, 1953**
The famous—some would say infamous—sheer gold lamé dress that Billy Travilla had to literally sew Marilyn into at the 1953 *Photoplay* awards.

Another dress that became one of the best-known costumes in film history was the simple halter-fronted off-white summer dress with sunburst pleats that Travilla designed for Marilyn to wear in *The Seven Year Itch.* It featured in the sequence where the skirt is blown up over Marilyn's shoulders as she stands on a subway grating with a train passing below. The image rendered Marilyn Monroe an icon almost overnight.

Travilla, who died in 1990, worked as closely with Marilyn as almost anyone in her career. "On the surface she was still a happy girl. But those who criticized her never saw her as I did, crying like a baby because she often felt herself so inadequate. Sometimes she suffered terrific depressions, and would even talk about death."

And their regard for each other was mutual, Marilyn famously autographing a copy of her nude calendar with the message "Billy dear, please dress me forever. I love you, Marilyn."

*Left:* **New York, September 15, 1954**
Wearing a similarly pleated dress to the Travilla number Marilyn is wearing (and about to make famous), is actress Gina Lollobrigida. Known as "Italy's Marilyn Monroe," she met her US counterpart the day Marilyn was shooting the "billowing dress" location scene for *The Seven Year Itch.*

*Right:* **On stage in Korea, February 1954**

On February 16, 1954, Marilyn interrupted her honeymoon with Joe DiMaggio in Japan, to fly to the Korean capital Seoul to visit—and perform for—US servicemen stationed in the country. Over the next four days she performed ten shows, in front of audiences that totalled more than 100,000 soldiers and marines. Marilyn was to treasure the memory of those concerts, admitting to her friend Amy Greene that they were "the best thing that ever happened to me. I never felt like a star before in my heart. It was so wonderful to look down and see a fellow smiling at me."

# Gee. I never thought I had an effect on people until I was in Korea.

*Left:* **Korea, February 1954**
At every concert that Marilyn
Monroe gave in Korea she was
surrounded by adoring
servicemen, even signing copies
of her nude calendar for some
lucky troopers.

*Left:* **Hollywood, 1953**

Marilyn with one of her biggest—and most influential—fans, the Hollywood columnist Louella Parsons, who seemed to champion the star as if she was simply beyond criticism in everything she did. Her column and radio show were almost evangelical in their enthusiasm for the actress.

It is Marilyn who is number one on all the GI polls of Hollywood favorites, and number one on exhibitors' polls of box office favorites. She is the number one cover girl of the year, and certainly number one in public interest wherever she goes.

**Louella Parsons**

> **Marilyn's a phenomenon of nature, like Niagara Falls and the Grand Canyon. All you can do is stand back and be awed by it.**
>
> **Nunnally Johnson, producer**

## ★ How To Marry A Millionaire

Another "gold digger" theme, this time with three females on the track of marital millions, It was one of the first films shot in Fox's new widescreen format, Cinemascope.

Studio: 20th Century Fox
Released: November 1953
Producer: Nunnally Johnson

Director: Jean Negulesco
Format: Cinemascope and Technicolor
Leads: Betty Grable, Marilyn Monroe, Lauren Bacall

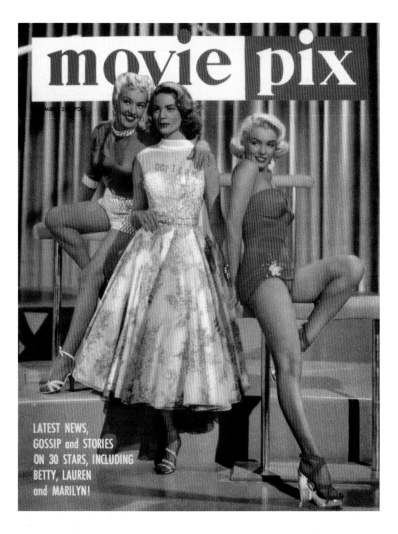

# movie pix

**LATEST NEWS, GOSSIP and STORIES ON 30 STARS, INCLUDING BETTY, LAUREN and MARILYN!**

*Left:* **Fox publicity, November 1953**
In a figure-hugging gown designed for her by Billy Travilla, Marilyn gives
the camera her come-hither look in this Fox publicity shot for the release
of *How To Marry A Millionaire*.

*Above:* **How To Marry A Millionaire, 1953**
Aboard a luxuriously appointed passenger jet, Marilyn's gold-digger Pola
goes to work on suave rich man, J. Steward Merrill, played by Alex D'Arcy.

She represents to man something we all want in our unfulfilled dreams. A man, he's got to be dead not to be excited by her.

**Jean Negulesco, director**

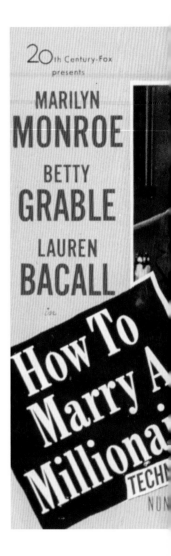

*Right:* **Front of house picture, How To Marry A Millionaire, 1953** The film was one of the first in the wide-screen Cinemascope process— which you see without glasses—and gets bigger billing than the stars.

CinemaScope — YOU SEE IT WITHOUT GLASSES!

David WAYNE · Rory CALHOUN · Cameron MITCHELL · ALEX D'ARCY FRED CLARK · and WILLIAM POWELL

NSON · JEAN NEGULESCO · NUNNALLY JOHNSON

Directed by    Screen Play by

Based on Plays by Zoe Akins, Dale Eunson and Katherine Albert

# The Jack Benny Show

Testament to Marilyn's star status by September 1953 was an appearance, her first on TV, on the prestigious *Jack Benny Show*. Benny was an institution in American show business, playing, as always, the tight-fisted character that became his trademark—an off-screen "third voice" in his head accompanying his chirpy dialogue in a sketch with Marilyn.

MM: In the picture, all I wanted was money and diamonds, but now for the first time, I realize that all I really want is you.

**JB: Marilyn. Marilyn, I'm mad about you.**

MM: I'm mad about you too Jack. Jack—will you do something wonderful for me? It would make me very happy.

**JB: Well, of course, Marilyn. I'd do anything, anything for you. What is it?**

MM: Well, in my next picture there's going to be so many love scenes, I want you for my leading man.

**JB: Oh Marilyn, I'd love to be your leading man.**

MM: Good. Now if we can only get permission from Darryl Zanuck.

**JB: Why? Who did Mr Zanuck have in mind?**

MM: Himself!

**JB: Gee Marilyn. I just can't get over the both of us here all alone.**

MM: Yes Jack. I never dreamed it could happen to I.

**JB: Neither did me.**

*MARILYN SIGHS.*

**JB: Marilyn, why are you sighing?**

MM: I was just thinking Jack, how generous you are. Just so we could be alone on this trip, you chartered this [yacht] for $600,000.

**JB: I did?**

*VOICE OVER: If that doesn't wake him up, nothing will!*

**JB: Marilyn, Marilyn. I know this is sudden, but will you marry me?**

MM: Marry? But look at the difference in our ages.

**JB: Well, there isn't much difference Marilyn. You're 25 and I'm 39.**

MM: Yes, but what about 25 years from now, when I'm 50 and you're 39?

**JB: Gee, I never thought of that.**

*VOICE OVER: I did!*

**JB: You shut up! Marilyn... Marilyn will you have dinner with me tonight?**

MM: Oh I'd love to Jack. Thanks ever so.

**JB: At 8 o'clock?**

MM: Alright, but I better be going now.

*MARILYN SINGS "BYE BYE BABY" AND THEY KISS.*

*Above:* **The Jack Benny Show, September 13, 1953**
Jack Benny and Marilyn in the sketch that ends with a kiss that leaves
Marilyn somewhat cold and Benny, as he put it, "a wreck."

# Escapist Cinema and the Cold War

The career of Marilyn Monroe spanned a social era dominated, especially in America, by the Cold War, the "red scare" years which had a profound impact on popular culture generally and Hollywood in particular.

The most sinister by-product of the nuclear stand-off between the United States and the Soviet Union was undoubtedly McCarthyism, in which Senator Joseph McCarthy's HUAC—the House Committee on UnAmerican Activities—searched for covert Communists in every corner of American life, the popular media being a popular target.

So it was that the notorious "hearings" ensued, in which individuals appearing before the Committee were asked to confess to any associations with the Communist Party and name those who they also suspected of the same. Among the famous Hollywood names who resisted this coercion at the risk of going to jail were Humphrey Bogart and Lauren Bacall, Danny Kaye, Groucho Marx, Gene Kelly, Frank Sinatra, and many more.

Throughout her career Marilyn counted among her friends people of this liberal-leaning fraternity; her most creative and fulfilling periods of work were those when she rubbed shoulders with the similarly "progressive" company of individuals such as John Huston, Billy Wilder, and Lee Strasberg and others at the New York Actors' Studio. Her husband-to-be, Arthur Miller, was called to "name names" to the Committee in 1956, which he refused to do. His and Marilyn's fame (and popularity) was such that the State Department was forced to intervene on their behalf.

This period also saw a demand for "escapist" films that allowed the moviegoer to forget the perceived threat of a Communist takeover or nuclear annihilation, or analogized that threat in the "us-versus-them" paranoia of B-movie science fiction.

The movies, by their very nature, had always dealt in escapism, of course, no more so than in the sparkling Busby Berkeley musicals of the 1930s and 1940s that provided a glamorous respite from the daily rigors of the Depression and then the war.

Most of Marilyn's starring movies, from the glitzy comedy of *Gentlemen Prefer Blondes* to romantic romps like *Let's Make Love,* can be seen as part of this escapist tradition. Even in the Western settings of *River of No Return* and *Bus Stop* her roles allowed her to get up and sing a song or two as chorus girl or saloon-bar floozie; similairly, the very plots of *The Prince and the Showgirl*, *The Seven Year Itch* and *Some Like It Hot*—however diverting the comedy— could be said to be fantasist in the extreme. Only the thrillers *Don't Bother To Knock* and *Niagara*, both early on in her career as a lead star, had her in "hard-boiled" roles. By and large her movies—like her va-va-voom image right from the days of her earliest pinup photographs—were the stuff of fantasy and escapism.

But the 1950s also saw a new realism, exemplified in gritty dramas like *On The Waterfront*, *Rebel Without A Cause* and *The Sweet Smell of Success*. These films addressed the real issues concerning society and human relationships rather than giving their audience an escape route from them. It was, ironically, in her final film *The Misfits* that Marilyn was cast—in a role written for her by Arthur Miller—in a vehicle that reflected an alternative Hollywood. A Hollywood where, one suspects, her ambitions as a serious actress would have had a chance to develop even further.

It's a toss-up whether the scenery or the adornment of Marilyn Monroe is the feature of greater attraction in River Of No Return. The mountainous scenery is spectacular, but so in her own way is Miss Monroe.

**Bosley Crowther, New York Times**

## ★ River Of No Return

Western drama, with Marilyn and Mitchum escaping from warring Indians on a raft over the rapids.

**Studio:** 20th Century Fox
**Released:** April 1954
**Producer:** Stanley Rubin

**Director:** Otto Preminger
**Format:** Cinemascope and Technicolor
**Leads:** Robert Mitchum, Marilyn Monroe

*Above:* **Still, River Of No Return, 1954**

A scene from the frontier drama, as Marilyn's Kay Weston divides her attention between young Mark Calder (Tommy Rettig) and his father Matt played by screen tough guy, Robert Mitchum.

*Right:* **Hollywood, 1953**

Marilyn and co-star Robert Mitchum at a Hollywood function after the location shooting of *River Of No Return* in the Canadian Rockies.

# Marilyn and DiMaggio

When Marilyn Monroe met Joe DiMaggio, she was the rising star and he had retired the previous year (due to injuries) as the biggest baseball name in America. A native of San Francisco, his professional home for the peak years of his career had been the Yankee Stadium in the Bronx, New York, home of the New York Yankees where he had earned the nickname "the Yankee Clipper" due to his prowess with the bat. He was thirty-seven, Marilyn twenty-five.

Introduced via a friend, their first date was in March 1952, just around the time that the nude calendar story had broken in the press. Although it soon transpired that Joe frowned on some of the more sexually titillating aspects of Marilyn's image—at least when they were a bona fide item and the green-eyed monster of jealousy reared its head—the calendar scandal clearly didn't phase him right then. The pair were soon virtually inseparable, and the media loved it.

As did the general public. Now she was going out with a national sporting hero, Marilyn was a household name even among folk who didn't read the movie magazines. It certainly didn't do her public image any harm, and already married-and-divorced Joe was happy to go along with it, enjoying an enhanced profile as an all-American hero just as he was embarking on a well-earned retirement from the game. As it was, when they went out together, as much attention was often paid to him as to her—as sportsman and beautiful actress, they were a winning combination.

DiMaggio, from an Italian family steeped in the traditional values associated with the "old country," had a predictably conservative view of how women should behave and be treated. Although he was besotted with the beauty who was now "his" girl, with that came a possessiveness that at best was highly protective and at worst sparked with jealousy. And as Marilyn, over the next couple of years, became the most famous (and desired) woman in the world, so Joe DiMaggio became even more protective or jealous as the occasion demanded.

The essence of their seemingly unlikely relationship was that Joe was one of those "men's men," a guy more inclined to hang out with buddies in a bar than go shopping with his wife, to sit in front of the television all evening rather than help in the kitchen. Yet he would also "do anything" for the woman he was absolutely devoted to. Her champion.

He constantly warned her of the sharks and phonies he felt she was surrounded by in Hollywood, and would consciously try to bring her "down to earth" for what he felt was her own good. Others around Marilyn deemed this as patronizing in reverse, a boorish attitude that took no account of—or indeed understood—the world of actors and agents, writers and directors, photographers and publicists that was part of the essential fabric of his wife's life. With or without the inevitable hangers-on.

Despite these contradictions in their relationship, after they had been seeing each other for nearly two years they were married. The marriage took place on January 14, 1954, at a ceremony in the San Francisco City Hall in front of a handful of DiMaggio's close friends and family and none of Marilyn's.

*Next page:* **San Francisco City Hall, January 14, 1954**
Marilyn and Joe emerge from their civil wedding ceremony with the media, as always, in attendance. It was a presence that Joe was to find more and more difficult to live with throughout their brief marriage.

The subsequent "honeymoon" was not without its problems. It started with the press conferences, when Joe was visibly uncomfortable about questions to Marilyn about her views on sex, her sleeping arrangements, even her walk: "I learned to walk as a baby and I haven't had a lesson since."

Followed closely by the world's press, Joe mixed business with pleasure at pre-arranged exhibition games for the baseball-crazy Japanese, while Marilyn took off for her now-famous series of concerts in front of US troops in Korea. It was one of many occasions when Joe was less than happy about men paying attention to his wife.

The marriage, unlike their two-year courtship, was short-lived. After the Far East trip things got worse, with arguments—almost always centered on some aspect of Marilyn's career—that started to become violent, friends alleging Marilyn would be hiding bruises from time to time. A catalyst in all this came when Joe was witness to the "skirt blowing" sequence being staged for *The Seven Year Itch* on Lexington Avenue in New York before hundreds of delighted onlookers. Not long after the violent quarrel that followed, Marilyn filed a petition for divorce in October 1954, which was eventually granted a year later, in November 1955.

Joe DiMaggio, however, proved a longer-lasting friend than he had husband, being there for Marilyn when she most needed him, particularly during the traumatic final couple of years of her life. In the words of Allan "Whitey" Snyder, Marilyn's make-up artist for most of her career: "Joe DiMaggio was the best friend Marilyn ever had. They were no good married, but that's the way it goes with thousands of men and women."

*Above:* **"On the QT" magazine, 1955**

Although DiMaggio was used to the glare of publicity, the sensationalist press aimed at his wife was a contributing factor in their parting.

He didn't like the actors kissing me, and he didn't like my costumes. He didn't like anything about my movies, and he hated all my clothes. When I told him I had to dress the way I did, that it was part of my job, he said I should quit that job.

*Left:* **New York, June 1, 1955**
Despite their separation, Joe DiMaggio and Marilyn attended the premier of *The Seven Year Itch* together on Marilyn's twenty-ninth birthday.

*Above and right:* **508 North Palm Drive, Beverly Hills, October 6, 1954**
A tearful Marilyn, accompanied by her attorney, Gerry Giesler, outside the
DiMaggio Beverly Hills home, announcing the filing of her divorce before
being driven away (right) still visibly distraught. Although Giesler insisted
his client had nothing to say, pressed by over a hundred reporters and
photographers Marilyn sobbed before getting in the car: "I can't say
anything today. I'm sorry, I'm so sorry."

*Above:* **Santa Monica Court, October 27, 1954**

In the courtroom with lawyer Giesler as the divorce proceedings get under way. Marilyn was adamant she wanted a divorce, even though Joe DiMaggio attempted a reconciliation. Dressed in a smart black outfit and white pearl necklace, she ended her statement to the judge with an emotional summing up: "I hoped to have out of my marriage, love, warmth, affection, and understanding. But the relationship was mostly one of coldness and indifference."

*Above:* **Cedars of Lebanon Hospital, November 12, 1954**
After five days at the Los Angeles Cedars of Lebanon Hospital, being treated for her chronic endometriosis, Marilyn left via a back entrance so as not to be noticed, only to be greeted by some highly intrusive paparazzi, mainly from the New York *Daily News*. Despite the impending divorce, her constant visitor during her brief stay was DiMaggio, fuelling press speculation that they had, after all, patched things up. Marilyn assured the world that wasn't the case, but added that they would always be friends.

# ★ There's No Business Like Show Business

Spectacular show-biz-based musical with songs by Irving Berlin. Marilyn played night club singer Vicky, delivering a rendition of "Heat Wave."

Studio: 20th Century Fox
Released: December 1954
Producer: Sol C. Siegel

Director: Walter Lang
Format: Cinemascope and color by DeLuxe
Leads: Ethel Merman, Dan Dailey, Donald O'Connor, Marilyn Monroe, Johnnie Ray

*Left:* **On set with Johnnie Ray, summer 1954**

Marilyn and singer Johnnie Ray relax on the *Show Business* set. Ray, known as the "Cry Guy" on account of his tearful on-stage histrionics, was a huge star in the early 1950s, prior to the advent of rock'n'roll.

*Next page:* **There's No Business Like Show Business, 1954**

A movie which many considered little more than an excuse for lavish production numbers. Left to right, Ethel Merman, Dan Dailey, Mitzi Gaynor, Donald O'Connor, and Marilyn in costume for her "Heat Wave" sequence.

# Marilyn Sings

Marilyn sings! The image that comes immediately to mind is the spectacular "Diamonds Are A Girl's Best Friend" set-piece in *Gentlemen Prefer Blondes*—but Marilyn's vocalising, sensational though it was in that number, had a lot more to it than that.

As early in her career as 1948, when she sang two songs as part of her chorus girl role in *Ladies of the Chorus*, she exhibited a smoky voiced style that was uniquely Marilyn, with the trade paper *Motion Picture Herald* describing her singing as one of the bright spots in the movie. Another early chorus girl part, in the western comedy *A Ticket To Tomahawk*, featured her as one of four hoofers singing "Oh, What A Forward Young Man!" But, as with many aspects of her early career, Marilyn decided that if anything was to be done about her singing, she had better do it herself.

Always a fan of the great jazz vocalists—particularly Ella Fitzgerald whose records she would listen to over and over again, into the small hours of the morning—Marilyn began taking singing lessons from studio musician Hal Schaefer during 1952. She once told the vocal coach "I won't be satisfied until people want to hear me sing without looking at me."

Following her initial sessions with Schaefer she appeared before troops as part of a studio-sponsored entertainment program, performing a show-stopping version of a 1922 Broadway hit "Do It Again." The record she made of the song in January 1953 was an erotically charged—though initially unavailable—classic; likewise with "Kiss," which she sings just a portion of in *Niagara*. Had the full recording been available then, there would have been a different assessment of Marilyn as singer. But only a snippet appeared in the film, the commercial disc remaining unreleased until after her death.

*Above:* **Tiffany Club, Hollywood, November 17, 1954**
Marilyn's biggest musical idol was jazz singer, Ella Fitzgerald. She once secured a booking for the singer in a previously white-only nightclub, the Mocambo, by promising to take a front row table every night Ella played. "She was ahead of her time, and she didn't know it," Ella recalled years later.

# I won't be satisfied until people want to hear me sing without looking at me.

*Above:* **"Diamonds Are A Girl's Best Friend," spring 1953**
With a chorus of admiring males, Marilyn gives it her all in her trademark song from *Gentlemen Prefer Blondes*.

*Right:* **"After You Get What You Want, You Don't Want It," summer, 1954**
A spectacular set-piece—albeit in a movie full of glitzy set-pieces and little else—was this sequence from *There's No Business Like Show Business*.

# I think she was a better singer than most professional singers. She worked hard and was always on time.

## Lionel Newman, songwriter and musical director

The first real indication of just how accomplished Marilyn's vocal style was came in her next movie, *Gentlemen Prefer Blondes*. Here her breathy, husky vibrato and jazz-tinged phrasing were used to dynamic effect in two duets with Jane Russell—"Bye Bye Baby" and "Two Little Girls From Little Rock"—and what became her unofficial signature tune, "Diamonds Are A Girl's Best Friend."

Now her singing was accepted and indeed seen as a bonus factor by the studio. Even in movies which had no musical context whatsoever, a situation would be created to accommodate a vocal spot, as in *River Of No Return,* a western drama in which she happens to be a bar room singer—cue the title song, "One Silver Dollar," and "I'm Gonna File My Claim."

*There's No Business Like Show Business,* on the other hand, was all about show-biz and music, in which some unmemorable numbers were eclipsed by Marilyn's "After You Get What You Want You Don't Want It" and a torrid rendition of "Heat Wave."

She was back singing in that saloon again in the modern western *Bus Stop* with a sizzling version of the standard "That Old Black Magic," complete with an Oklahoma accent! But with 1959's *Some Like It Hot* she came up with another trademark number,

*Left:* **"River Of No Return," fall, 1953**
As the sultry voiced saloon-bar vocalist, Kay Weston, Marilyn wows the locals with her voice—and outfit no doubt—in *River Of No Return*.

the 1920s-style "ooo-poo-pe-doo" in "I Want To Be Loved By You" that was pure Marilyn in every way.

And though it met with mixed reviews, critics and audiences alike agreed that the greatest moment in *Let's Make Love*—no, not her duet with the English pop balladeer Frankie Vaughan (surely the least likely casting in all of Marilyn's films)—was her sexually loaded version of "My Heart Belongs To Daddy."

No account of Marilyn's singing can go without mention of her brief but legendary rendition of "Happy Birthday, Mr President" to John F. Kennedy and 15,000 supporters. Not long before her death, her voice sounded both nervous and sure of itself at the same time, a final hint that Marilyn, the singer, might—like Marilyn, the actress—have given us even more had circumstances been different.

*Right:* "**Runnin' Wild," fall, 1958**
The railroad journey sequence from *Some Like It Hot*. Marilyn, as Sugar Kane, sashays down the aisle with her ukulele while Tony Curtis and Jack Lemmon as "Josephine" and "Daphne" can be seen at the back of the carriage playing tenor sax and double bass respectively.

## chapter 4

# Divorce, the Method, and Miller

# "She is pure cinema" 1954–58

The sophisticated comedy *The Seven Year Itch*, from a stage play
by George Axelrod, marked another milestone in Marilyn's career.
The part certainly required a sexy, breathy female, but Marilyn's
performance under the guidance of director Billy Wilder seemed to
be a subtle send-up of her previous "dumb blonde" stereotypes.
Plus, of course, there was the famous "white dress" sequence in
which Marilyn stands over a New York subway grating, the wind from
which blows her garment up over her shoulders. The sequence,
which was staged in the Hollywood studio to get it exactly right, had
already been shot on September 15, 1954, on the actual Manhattan
streets, as an event to generate publicity. It was witnessed by
hundreds of delighted spectators.

One onlooker who was not so delighted was her overtly jealous
husband, Joe DiMaggio, and his reaction to this incident proved to
be the culmination of difficulties that led to their eventual divorce.

Meanwhile, Marilyn, on completing the film in November, was
guest of honor at Romanoff's Restaurant in Beverly Hills attended by
the cream of Hollywood high society. A souvenir portrait presented
to her was signed by the assembled well-wishers who included
Humphrey Bogart and Lauren Bacall, William Holden, James
Stewart, Gary Cooper, Doris Day, and Marilyn's childhood idol Clark
Gable—plus the "big three" of Hollywood moguls: Jack Warner,
Sam Goldwyn, and Darryl F. Zanuck.

In December 1954, Marilyn Monroe, by this time the most
celebrated movie star in the world, took the unprecedented step of
a self-imposed "exile" which was to last until the end of the following
year. Rejecting Fox's proposal for her next film, *How To Be Very,
Very Popular* in which she was to play a stripper, Marilyn retreated

to the Connecticut home of photographer Milton H. Greene and his wife Amy. Greene was already becoming something of a guiding light for Marilyn: "I feel deeply about him. I'm sincere about his genius. He's a genius." On December 31 she founded Marilyn Monroe Productions Inc. with Greene. Greene promised to sort out her difficulties with 20th Century Fox once and for all.

Crucially, the move East also brought her into more regular orbit with the man who she first met when she was shooting *As Young As You Feel* in 1951: the playwright, Arthur Miller.

The Greenes also had a 52nd Street apartment in New York City, which Marilyn was able to utilize as she pleased. After the often stifling social milieu of Hollywood, life in Manhattan—as often as possible with the already married Miller—was like a breath of fresh air. She was, nevertheless, undergoing increasing bouts of psychiatric treatment, which had started in 1954.

As if to emphasize her demarcation from Fox, Marilyn announced at a press conference set up by Greene that she hoped to play the part of Grushenka in a film version of Dostoevsky's *The Brothers Karamazov*. The studio were quick to point out that her contract had another three years to run, and there was no question of their granting her request.

She may have exiled herself from Hollywood and actual movie-making, but through 1955 Marilyn was no recluse. Publicity opportunities ensured her profile remained as high as ever, from an appearance riding a pink-painted elephant at a charity "circus" event in Madison Square Garden to the more serious TV interview with Edward R. Murrow in his *Person To Person* series, which attracted more than 50 million viewers.

Confirming the seriousness with which she approached her acting—no doubt influenced by Arthur Miller—Marilyn enrolled at the

214

prestigious Actors' Studio run by Lee Strasberg. The home of the "Method school" of acting—with which she was already familiar via her seven years with drama coach Natasha Lytess—it had been the launch pad for a new breed of actors of the period, including Marlon Brando, James Dean, Paul Newman, Montgomery Clift, and her co-star from *The Seven Year Itch*, Tom Ewell.

After twelve months in the pipeline, Marilyn's divorce from Joe DiMaggio was finally granted in November 1955, followed at the end of the year by a reconciliation with Fox. Following the huge success of her last picture, Zanuck agreed with Marilyn and Milton Greene to a new contract giving her the right of refusal on any film proposal she considered unsuitable, and flexibility to pursue her own projects. In other words, she had the artistic freedom she required to pursue her ambitions as a serious actress.

In February 1956, Marilyn pursued those ambitions, albeit in a modest way, and drew an enthusiastic response at the Actors' Studio in a performance of a scene from Eugene O'Neill's *Anna Christie*.

That same month she announced at a press conference, accompanied by the most famous figure on the British stage, Sir Laurence Olivier, that the latter would be directing her in a film version of the Terence Rattigan play *The Sleeping Prince*.

Meanwhile, Hollywood beckoned once again, and in May 1956 shooting commenced on *Bus Stop*. From a Broadway play by William Inge, it was the first project Marilyn selected herself under her new contract with Fox; she also chose director, Joshua Logan.

*Left:* **Los Angeles Airport, February 25, 1956**
Marilyn chats with friend and business partner, Milton Greene. Of their new arrangement with Fox, *Time* magazine commented "Last week as the battle ended, the clear winner was Marilyn Monroe Productions Inc."

Arthur Miller, now divorced, finally married Marilyn on June 29, after which she gasped to the press, "This is the first time I've been really in love. Arthur is a serious man, but he has a wonderful sense of humor. We laugh and joke a lot. I'm mad about him."

Instead of a honeymoon, the couple soon found themselves in London, their arrival heralded by a press conference also attended by Olivier, to mark the beginning of work on the planned film, now entitled *The Prince and the Showgirl*. England, and the British media particularly, was all agog at the arrival of the almost legendary sex symbol, with the press re-running every "blonde bombshell" cliché in the book.

Madness of another kind threatened to break out on the movie set at Pinewood Studios, as Marilyn's notorious stage fright and memory lapses—plus the alien nuances of her Actors' Studio training—clashed with the "stage" formalism of the British theatrical establishment as represented by Olivier and others. For Marilyn, the friction was often palpable, her personal psychiatrist having to be flown over from New York to deal with frequent traumas.

The star exhibited increasingly erratic behavior, resulting in part to the end, in early 1957, of her partnership—and friendship—with Milton Greene. Greene nevertheless continued to defend her in public: "All I did was believe in her. She was a marvelous, loving, wonderful person I don't think many people understood."

This was followed in August 1957 by an emotional crisis prompted by the loss of a baby after two months of pregnancy. It was to be another year before Marilyn set foot on a film set again, for what would become her most celebrated comedy vehicle of all, the Billy Wilder-directed *Some Like It Hot*.

*Above:* **Poster, The Seven Year Itch, France, 1955**

Marilyn's popularity in France, where film is considered a prime art form, was rivaled only by that of their homegrown sex kitten, Brigitte Bardot.

*Next page:* **Romanoff's Restaurant, Beverly Hills, November 1955**

With Humphrey Bogart (left) and Clifton Webb during the star-studded Hollywood reception celebrating the release of *The Seven Year Itch*.

*Above and right:* **Madison Square Garden, March 30, 1955**

In March 1955, Marilyn took part in a benefit for the Arthritis and Rheumatism Association, at the opening night of Ringling Brothers' Circus at Madison Square Garden, organized by impresario Mike Todd and Milton Greene. It subsequently appeared on the cover of *Pic* magazine trailing a piece on her "embarrassing moment." Marilyn entered the arena on a pink-painted Indian elephant, confessing on TV the following week: "It meant a lot to me because I'd never been to the circus as a kid."

*Left:* **With Edward R. Murrow, April 8, 1955**
Marilyn took part in the *Person to Person* CBS
TV interview show with prestigious journalist
Murrow, broadcast live from Milton and Amy
Greene's home in Connecticut. At first terrified
by the prospect, she predictably became more
relaxed once the cameras began rolling.

It's not that I object to doing
musicals and comedies—in
fact, I rather enjoy them—
but I'd like to do dramatic
parts, too.

**Marilyn Monroe to Edward R. Murrow**

Screen stories

JULY 20¢

DELL MAGAZINE

"The Seven Year Itch"

starring

Marilyn Monroe & Tom Ewell

# ★ The Seven Year Itch

Marilyn plays "The Girl Upstairs" in a comedy concerning a husband, Tom Ewell, who, while his wife is away, fantasizes about the beautiful blonde who lives in the apartment above.

Studio: 20th Century Fox
Released: June 1955
Producer: Charles K. Feldman and Billy Wilder

Director: Billy Wilder
Format: Cinemascope and color by DeLuxe
Leads: Tom Ewell, Marilyn Monroe

# I'd have been upset, you know, if there were 20,000 people watching my wife's skirt blow over her head.

**Billy Wilder**

*Previous page:* **Hollywood, September 1954**
Billy Wilder directing the famous scene in *The Seven Year Itch* with Marilyn and Tom Ewell, reshot in Hollywood having first being staged on location in New York in the glare of press photographers and onlookers.

*Right:* **Lexington Avenue, New York City, September 1954**
Photographer Sam Shaw was credited with the original idea of an open shoot on location in New York, which did much for the film's publicity.

The four-story-high billboard for *The Seven Year Itch*, at Loew's State Theater in New York's Times Square, said it all. The "dress blowing" image of Marilyn had rendered her an icon like no other before or since.

There was my name up in lights. I said, "God, somebody's made a mistake." But there it was, in lights. And I sat there and said, "Remember, you're not a star." Yet there it was, up in lights.

# Marilyn and the Method

Marilyn Monroe was very much a product, and some would say
victim, of the Hollywood star system that had held sway in the film
capital since the days of the silent movies. It was a regime in which
the big studio moguls—men like Sam Goldwyn, Louis B. Mayer,
Jack Warner, and in Marilyn's case, Daryl F. Zanuck—and their
hierarchical organizations, had absolute power over the actors and
actresses under their contractual control.

Decisions about which roles to accept, publicity activity, even
matters concerning their private life, were ultimately out of the hands
of the individuals concerned for the duration of their contract. It
applied to directors, screenwriters, and other creative film folk to a
lesser degree, but it was the stars who the studios felt they had
"created" that were most at the mercy of the system.

Marilyn, however, unlike predecessors such as Mae West or
Jean Harlow, came along at a time when things were beginning to
change. Alongside the magical musicals and escapist adventures
that traditionally sustained the cinema industry, the 1950s saw new,
grittier "realistic" films starting to come out of Hollywood, and along
with them a new breed of so-called "Method" actors who would
eschew as far as possible the straitjacket of the star system. And
Marilyn's development as an actress, despite pictures that were in
the main "escapist," was directly influenced by her involvement with
the Method.

The Method style of acting was derived initially from the writings
and teachings of the Russian actor and director, Konstantin
Stanislavsky, and taken up in New York by the Actors' Studio which
was founded in 1947 by Cheryl Crawford, Robert Lewis, and Elia
Kazan. In 1951 Lee Strasberg (who had trained as an actor in

*Above:* **With Lee Strasberg, date unknown**

Marilyn at a dinner event with Method school mentor Lee Strasberg (right) who, with, his wife Paula, remained an influence throughout her career.

New York in the 1920s with Richard Boleslawski, an ex-colleague of Stanislavsky at the Moscow Arts Theatre) was made artistic director of the Studio.

The basis of the style involved actors immersing themselves in a character by bringing to bear their own personality on a part, delving into their own emotional and psychological background in order to do so—even with the aid of psychoanalysis and therapy, if necessary.

Marilyn's enrolment at the Actors' Studio early in 1955, when she was already a huge star, was to give it (and Lee Strasberg) its biggest mass-circulation publicity. However, it was as the training ground for a whole stable of new actors that it impacted on the world of theater and, more significantly, cinema. Names including Marlon Brando, Paul Newman, Rod Steiger, Shelley Winters, James Dean, Montgomery Clift, Karl Malden, and Steve McQueen were all products of the Studio. These were names that were to change film acting forever.

Marilyn initially was a mere observer at her sessions at the Studio, but that was as important a part of the process as any. As she relaxed into the company of her fellow actors she opened up in the talk-through forums with opinions and critiques that she wouldn't have believed possible a few years before. And when she did run through scenes, as with her delivery from Eugene O'Neil's *Anna Christie* which had the normally reticent class wildly applauding, everyone was struck by the sheer presence she exuded on stage.

The actress Kim Stanley, who originated Marilyn's *Bus Stop* role on stage, recalled the occasion: "She was wonderful. We were

*Left:* **New York City, December 4, 1956**
Marilyn on the steps of the the Actors' Studio in New York.

taught never to clap at the Actors' Studio—it was like we were in church—and it was the first time I'd ever heard applause there."

With its introspective approach, and insistence that an actor had to give all emotionally, the Method in many ways found better application in film. Here, a scene could be repeated and repeated until the "right" feel and expression was reached—and certainly accommodated Marilyn's notorious on-set vacillations more easily than traditional stage discipline.

The influence of Lee Strasberg on Marilyn, and more directly that of his wife Paula as personal drama coach, was frequently resented by others close to her, from Joe DiMaggio (who didn't really understand what they were about) to Arthur Miller (who understood perfectly). Many have proffered the notion that the Method, or at least what she absorbed of it, was a useful crutch in the face of Marilyn's shortcomings as an actress. However, in retrospect it could also be seen as a stimulus that confirmed her instinct that she *wanted* to act, despite an innate lack of confidence in her own ability. It made an actress out of a star.

*Right:* **New York, March 9, 1955**
Marilyn, along with Marlon Brando, volunteered to act as usher at the premiere of *East of Eden* to benefit the Actors' Studio. The film, directed by Elia Kazan, was the launch pad for the tragically short career of another Actors' Studio alumnus, James Dean, who died later that same year.

*Above:* **Movie Stars Parade, February 1956**

Hollywood gossip magazines—like today's "celebrity" titles—linked the stars of the day in alleged affairs that often had no substance in fact. In the case of Marlon Brando, Marilyn was certainly seen around with him a lot through the latter part of 1955 and early 1956.

*Left:* **New York, December 1955**

Marilyn dances with Marlon Brando—probably the greatest of all the screen names to come out of the Actors' Studio—at a celebration party after the premiere of *The Rose Tattoo*.

I thought I'd seen them all; being in the business I'd seen so many models and actresses. But I'd never seen anyone with that tone of voice, that kindness, that real softness. If she saw a dead dog in the road, she'd cry. She was so supersensitive you had to watch your tone of voice all the time. Later I was to find out that she was schizoid—that she could be absolutely brilliant or absolutely kind, then the total opposite.

**Milton Greene**

*Right:* **Hollywood, March 1, 1956**
Milton Greene (left) and Marilyn with Warner Bros supremo Jack Warner —holding the key to Warner Bros Pictures—on the signing of their agreement for the film version of *The Sleeping Prince*.

# Everybody is always tugging at you. They'd all like a sort of chunk out of you.

*Left:* **Los Angeles, June 1956**

The president of Indonesia, Sukarno, chatting with Marilyn during a party given by *Bus Stop* director Joshua Logan and his wife at a Beverly Hills hotel. The party was given in honor of Logan's brother-in-law, Marshall Noble, who was traveling with the sixty-two members of the Indonesian party. Sukarno had specifically asked if he could meet Marilyn, who he said was one of the favorite actresses in his country.

# Interview with Ed Pfizenmaier

**ASSISTANT, CECIL BEATON**         New Jersey, February 17, 2004

**Early in 1956, the distinguished British society and celebrity photographer, Cecil Beaton, photographed Marilyn in a single session at the Ambassador Hotel in New York. He had a suite there at the time, which he had redecorated himself in what he described as a "Japanese Nouveau art manner." He had just started doing work for *Harper's Bazaar*, and the Marilyn shoot was one of a series that took place in the Hotel on Park Avenue featuring various celebrities who also included Joan Crawford and Maria Callas.**

**Unlike many photographers today, Beaton used just one assistant, and on his visits to New York this was usually Ed Pfizenmaier, who worked regularly as assistant to the fashion photographer, Horst.**

"It was called 'the King photographing the Queen,' or that's the way it was focussed on at the time. Whenever Beaton came to New York, which was periodically, I'd work with him, we'd work out of that site all the time because that's where he stayed. Cecil decorated the interior, remember he had many attributes, he was a painter, a photographer, an illustrator, set designer, interior designer.

"Anyway, suddenly Marilyn shows up with a simple black dress and a white puffy evening type thing, and that was it ... and we got to work immediately. And would you believe, she even did her own make-up which most people, they can't believe it nowadays ... but remember we're talking fifty years ago and things have changed radically. But she came just by herself, with these two little dresses and ... it was as simple as that.

"Contrary to what everyone says that she was difficult and hard to work with, I found her just a delight to work with, not difficult at all—I don't know where people come from—we just had a magnificent time. You have to attribute it to Beaton because he was the master, but she loved to be photographed ... you could feel it, you could see it with her.

"And she was smart enough to know about the value of publicity, and what it means, and to be photographed by Beaton especially, was basically what it was all about.

"I loved her sexuality, the glamour of it all, it was just fabulous. I thought Beaton's English wit mesmerized her totally ... and she was just like a purring she-lion under those lights. In those days we had tungsten lights ... today it's all popping strobes and everything, but in those days we had 10,000 watt bulbs, shining off the ceiling, which made a big difference to what it's like today."

**Beaton later described the session in his memoirs:**
*"She romps, she squeals with delight, she leaps on the sofa. She puts a flower stem in her mouth, puffing on a daisy as though it were a cigarette. It is an artless, impromptu, high-spirited performance. It will probably end in tears."*

**The description "artless" could be taken as meaning unpretentious, without airs or graces.**

"I couldn't agree more. I don't know if it was one of her better days, or a good day or what, you know you hear so many bad reports, the sensationalism, but I certainly didn't experience any of that. And I think the photographs, Beaton's photographs, show it, that's the proof of the pudding. When you look at them, everyone remarks she looks so happy, gay, healthy, and everything ... I think that is what Beaton brought out of her. She was totally relaxed all the time."

Marilyn Monroe calls to mind the bouquet of a firework display, eliciting from her awed spectators an open mouthed chorus of ohs and ahs. She is as spectacular as the silvery showers of a Vesuvius Fountain; she has rocketed from obscurity to become a post-war sex symbol—the pinup girl of an age.

**Cecil Beaton**

*Right and next page:* **Ambassador Hotel, New York, February 22, 1956**
Cecil Beaton working with Marilyn, photographed by Ed Pfizenmaier. One of the photographs from the shoot would subsequently appear as the centerpiece to a triptych presentation. The other two panels framed a hand-written eulogy to Marilyn by Beaton (an exert from which is quoted above), which director Joshua Logan presented to the star on the release of *Bus Stop* later that year.

# Marriage to Miller

Arthur Miller, ten years older than Marilyn Monroe, was thirty-five when they first met early in 1951. Born in New York in 1915 into a working class family, he'd experienced the poverty of the Depression first hand before graduating from high school to the University of Michigan. He went on to become one of the major names in American drama after his success with the plays *All My Sons* in 1947, and *Death of a Salesman* the following year.

He met Marilyn, already making a name for herself after well-received performances in *The Asphalt Jungle* and *All About Eve*, on the set of her eleventh movie, *As Young As You Feel*. The two of them were introduced by Elia Kazan. Like Miller, Kazan was already a big name on the contemporary stage, having been a co-founder of the Actors' Studio, and later as a Hollywood director with *A Streetcar Named Desire* and the film then in production *Viva Zapata!*, both starring the young Marlon Brando.

Miller first set eyes on Marilyn actually shooting a scene, as she was being tracked by a camera walking across a set representing a crowded nightclub room. That first image of her was to impress itself indelibly on his memory, as he recalled years later in his memoir, *Timebends*:

She was being shot from the rear to set off the swivelling of her hips, a motion fluid enough to seem comic. It was, in fact, her natural walk.

**Arthur Miller**

The immediate attraction was mutual. It was, however, unstated (or at least understated) by both for some time, as the already married Miller accompanied Marilyn and Kazan—who had embarked on a brief affair—on visits to the cinema, trips to the country, even meetings with fellow writers.

Clearly the spark that was ignited didn't go out, despite Marilyn's two-year courtship and then marriage to Joe DiMaggio. Just weeks after getting back from their Tokyo honeymoon, and despite her fondness for Joe, she was to confess to confidant Sidney Skolsky that her real ambition was to marry Arthur Miller.

The two were thrown together more closely when, her divorce papers with Joe DiMaggio already filed, Marilyn moved east to stay in the home of the Milton Greenes in Connecticut. This was at the end of 1954. She also spent as much time as possible at their Manhattan apartment on 52nd Street. During the next few months, Marilyn became more involved with the playwright, who by now had added the Tony Award-winning *The Crucible* to his literary laurels.

Miller fulfilled the intellectual void that Marilyn felt in her relationship with DiMaggio. Miller was a "serious" artist, and, like most intelligentsia in New York at the time he leant firmly to the liberal left. Although interested in what had been achieved in Soviet Russia, Miller was by no means an apologist for Communism, even though his sympathies may have inclined that way in his youth.

When it came to the crunch, Miller refused to name to the authorities others who like him might have once belonged to "unAmerican" organizations. This was to cause a rift with Elia Kazan, who notoriously did name people to Senator Joe McCarthy's House Committee on Un-American Activities. The FBI even opened a file on Marilyn because of her association with Miller, the Greenes, the Strasbergs—all liberal-minded "possible Communists"—and her

expressed interest in Russian literature and the Russian theater, fashionable at the time among actors and writers both in and outside the Actors' Studio.

On June 11, 1956, Arthur Miller was granted a divorce from his wife, Mary Grace Slattery. When he was summoned to appear before a HUAC hearing in Washington later that month, Miller used the occasion to make an emotional and articulate defense of free speech and civil liberties denied, he agreed, under Soviet Communism but also denied by the witch hunts of McCarthy: the very point he was making when he wrote *The Crucible*. Then, during the hearing, he requested that his confiscated passport be returned, announcing to the world that he planned to travel to England with "the woman who will then be my wife"—Marilyn Monroe. They were married in a civil ceremony on June 29, 1956.

In his own way, Miller turned out to be as protective of Marilyn as had Joe DiMaggio, but concerned more with her intellectual and professional well-being than the rival attention of Hollywood predators. As soon as they got to England to start shooting *The Prince and the Showgirl*, he found himself defending Marilyn not just against the sometimes superior attitude of Olivier, but also what he saw as the increasingly unnecessary presence of her drama coach, Paula Strasberg.

Indeed, he began to distance himself (and therefore Marilyn) from Lee and Paula Strasberg, upon whom he felt Marilyn had become too dependant, and Milton Greene, whom he increasingly

*Left:* **New York, June 22, 1956**
Marilyn hugs Arthur Miller during a sidewalk interview outside Greene's New York apartment. The couple denied reports that they would wed on June 23, stating that their marriage was planned for "some time in July."

suspected of ulterior motives regarding his wife. And even though she did split with Milton Greene, both business-wise and personally, Marilyn continued at the Actors' Studio and her association with the Strasbergs. Counter-productively from his point of view, some of the antagonisms that Miller opened up were beginning to rebound on their own relationship.

A further blemish on Marilyn's once-idealistic vision of her husband and what he stood for came when, in the middle of a strike by the Screen Actors Guild and Screen Writers Guild, he helped with some rewrites on *Let's Make Love*, in the face of the Hollywood rank and file who had managed to stop production on every other movie. Miller claimed in his autobiography that his motives were purely in support of Marilyn, to save her—and the movie—from "complete catastrophe … work I despised, on a script not worth the paper it was typed on."

More fundamental to the impending collapse of their marriage was Marilyn's affair with her *Let's Make Love* co-star Yves Montand, which developed while Arthur Miller was away from Hollywood, researching locations with John Huston for the film he had scripted and to be directed by Huston, *The Misfits*.

Being so closely involved in any film starring Marilyn would have put a strain on their relationship if her increasingly erratic behaviour with directors, writers, and fellow actors was anything to go by. The fact that *The Misfits* came, in 1960, when their marriage was falling apart could have only served to hasten their final separation. Marilyn's unreliability, the changes of mood, the reliance upon "outsiders" (crucially, Paula Strasberg), and increasing dependence on drugs and alcohol, now impacted on her relationship with Miller as both scriptwriter and husband.

When the film premiered on January 31, 1961, to mixed reviews, many critics saw the fraught relationships acted out against the barren black-and-white landscape as Miller's personal vision of their doomed partnership. The couple's divorce had been granted just days before, on January 20.

*Above:* **The Millers, July 1956**
Newlywed Marilyn with Arthur and in-laws, Isadore and Augusta Miller.

*Next page:* **Katonah, New York, July 1, 1956**
A Jewish wedding ceremony was held at the home of Miller's agent, Kay Brown.

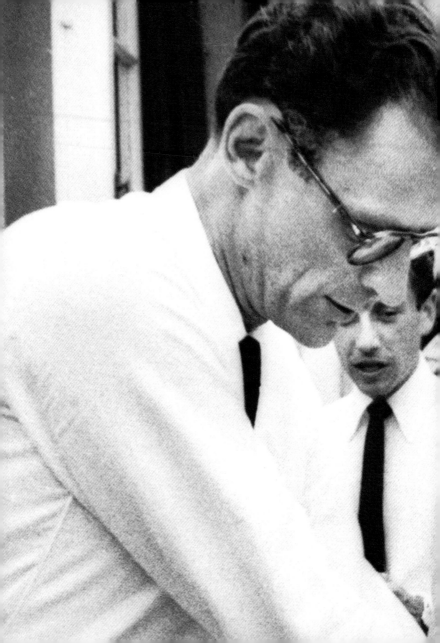

 **Bus Stop**

Another sex comedy concerning a simple-minded cowboy in Phoenix, Arizona, at rodeo time, who falls for Marilyn's Cherie, a saloon-bar singer.

Studio: 20th Century Fox
Released: August 1956
Producer: Buddy Adler

Director: Joshua Logan
Format: Cinemascope and color by DeLuxe
Leads: Marilyn Monroe, Don Murray

Marilyn is as near a genius as any actress I ever knew. She is an artist beyond artistry. She is the most completely realized and authentic film actress since Garbo. She has that same unfathomable mysteriousness. She is pure cinema.

**Joshua Logan, director, Bus Stop**

*Right:* **Phoenix, Arizona, 1956**
A publicity still of a rodeo scene from *Bus Stop*, shot by Milton Greene while the film was being made on location in Phoenix, Arizona.

# The knight and the actress

Right from the start, when contracts were signed between Marilyn Monroe Productions and Sir Laurence Olivier, the prospect of the world's biggest sex symbol and the man many considered the world's greatest actor joining forces on a movie was intriguing to say the least. The first official announcement came on February 7, 1956, in a press conference held in New York where Marilyn and Olivier met the media at the Plaza Hotel.

Accompanied by his agent, and the writer Terence Rattigan—whose play, *The Sleeping Prince,* they were to adapt for the screen—Olivier was clearly peeved when journalists elbowed him aside in their rush to get near the actress. In many ways, it was a portent of things to come. Likewise, when the strap on Marilyn's dress broke just as "Larry" was holding court, the latter was sure she'd contrived it to ensure the media spotlight stayed firmly on herself. His suspicions were confirmed later by designer John Moore, who dressed Marilyn for the occasion and was party to the "accident" being arranged in advance.

And the spotlight was certainly on Marilyn when she and Arthur Miller arrived in England prior to the actual shooting at Pinewood Studios, on July 13, 1956, just after the couple had got married. Although he was getting used to the attention lavished on his bride in public, even Miller was unprepared for their welcome at the airport, where they were besieged by hundreds of fans. He was to describe the ensuing mayhem as "a little like drowning, there was no air to breathe;" chaotic scenes followed, with a photographer crashing into a newsreel camera, knocking it over, with another pressman losing his balance and falling at Marilyn's feet.

Marilyn took it all in her stride, in fact with a coolness that some reporters interpreted as snobbish.

They were met at the airport by Sir Laurence and his wife, an astonished Vivien Leigh, who asked the American star if all her entrances were like this. "Well, this is a little quieter than some of them," Marilyn quickly replied.

What could only be described as Monroemania was sweeping Britain, led by a panting press coverage that ranged from the London *Evening News*'s "She's here, she walks, she talks, she really is as luscious as strawberries and cream!" to an ebullient acknowledgment of her beauty in the Communist *Daily Worker*. The next day another press conference took place, this time at the Savoy Hotel on London's Strand. Again, Marilyn managed to upstage Olivier, despite being an hour late, in an event that he described as one of the most embarrassing in his life. Before the cameras even started rolling, it looked as if *The Prince and the Showgirl* (as the film was to be called) was going to be a bumpy ride.

Once shooting at Pinewood did begin, with Mr. and Mrs. Miller ensconced in the grand Parkside House at Englefield Green, Windsor, the next bone of contention on the set—not for the first time—was the presence of Marilyn's drama coach from the Actors' Studio, Lee Strasberg's wife Paula. It further polarized Olivier's traditional theater-based view of how Marilyn should be dealing with her role, and the Method-school approach which was now an indelible feature of her style.

At the same time, like directors before him—who at least were used to a "Hollywood" way of handling such problems—he had to contend with Marilyn's continuing unreliability in terms of punctuality, memorizing lines, and generally "getting it right."

His solution was to be even more patronizing with Marilyn than

*Above:* **London Airport, July 14, 1956**
Sir Laurence Olivier and Vivien Leigh meeting Marilyn Monroe and
Arthur Miller on their arrival in London, July 14, 1956.

he might have been otherwise, referring to her as "a delightful little thing" to the other cast that included British stalwarts Richard Wattis and Dame Sybil Thorndike. A prime instance, in the first couple of days of shooting, was when he asked her to "try and be sexy."

She neither trusted or respected his judgment after that, and if anything, felt intimidated by him.

This was intensified when Vivien Leigh—not only an ex-Hollywood star who had appeared with Marilyn's hero Clark Gable in the 1939 epic *Gone With The Wind* but a sophisticated actress who had played Marilyn's "Showgirl" part on the stage—started appearing on the set, seemingly terrifying Marilyn with her air of authority.

One major crew member who did warm to Marilyn, and who apparently got the job at Marilyn's request if her not actual insistence, was the eminent cinematographer, Jack Cardiff.

"The fascinating thing about her was that I saw a lot of her, I used to go to her dressing room and talk to her and we became very good friends, and not once did I hear her swear. She had this kind of wondering look about her that was incredible, and there was never anything smutty about her and nothing cynical."

From the first it was evident that she was going to be a problem for Larry on the film. Most actors will come on the set and chat, but she would never come on the set. I felt quite sorry for Larry trying to act in and direct this film. She went through so many agonized times with Larry because he was, to her, a pain in the arse.

**Jack Cardiff**

Another ally on the film was fellow actress Dame Sybil Thorndike, who was, by this time, literally a legend of the English stage, yet who sensed that Marilyn had more of an innate feel for film acting than perhaps anyone else on the picture: "We need her desperately. She's the only one of us who really knows how to act in front of a camera."

Another grand English dame who took to Marilyn was the poet Edith Sitwell, inviting her to her home and discussing the work of Dylan Thomas, Gerald Manley Hopkins, and such, and who said of her, "She had a great natural dignity and was extremely intelligent. She was also exceedingly sensitive."

*Above:* **Comedy Theatre, London, October 18, 1956**
Sir Laurence and Lady Olivier—Vivien Leigh—with Marilyn and Arthur Miller, attending the first night of Miller's play *A View from the Bridge*.

And for all his condescension, Olivier conceded that she was a "natural" in front of the camera, be it in the movie studio or in front of the world's press. "Her work frightened her, and although she had undoubted talent, I think she had a subconscious resistance to the exercise of being an actress. But she was intrigued by its mystique and happy as a child when being photographed; she managed all the business of stardom with uncanny, clever, apparent ease."

Despite the trials and tribulations, *The Prince and the Showgirl* finished shooting at the end of October. It was not a great success either with the critics or at the box office, but Marilyn's performance did confirm Dame Sybil Thorndike's view. In his memoir of the making of the picture, *The Prince, the Showgirl and Me*, third assistant director Colin Clark recalled:

Despite [Olivier's] unprintable comments about her inexperience and unprofessionalism, Marilyn had appeared in virtually the same number of films as he had (The Prince and the Showgirl was her twenty-fifth to his twenty-eighth) and her relationship with the camera was more intimate than his —Dame Sybil was right. Watching the film today, Marilyn appears happy and natural, while Olivier often looks stiff and awkward.

A postscript to the making of the film, before the end of her five-month stay in Britain, was when Marilyn got to talk to real royalty. She was invited to meet Queen Elizabeth II at a Royal Film Performance at the Empire Theatre in Leicester Square on October 29, 1956. Prior to a screening of *The Battle of the River Plate*, an array of stars lined up to meet the monarch, including two European sex symbols of the time, Brigitte Bardot and Anita Ekberg, and Hollywood stars Joan Crawford and Victor Mature. The Queen had

*Right:* **Savoy Hotel, London, July 15, 1956**
Marilyn signing a photograph during the London press conference for *The Prince and the Showgirl* at the Savoy Hotel.

clearly been briefed as to where the Millers were staying: "You are my neighbor, Miss Monroe, how do you like living at Windsor?"

Marilyn was slightly confused, "I don't understand, I thought we lived at Englefield Green and you lived at Buckingham Palace?"

The Queen explained, "We often live at Windsor Castle and that makes us neighbors, doesn't it? So what do you think of the place'?"

"Oh, I think I see what you mean. Windsor Park, yes Windsor's a lovely place. We have a permit to bicycle in … in your park!" (She and Arthur Miller had been presented with bicycles by the *Daily Sketch* newspaper on their arrival in the country.)

Then Marilyn did a perfect curtsey.

"That's a very proper curtsey," the Queen said.

"Curtseying isn't difficult for me now. I learned how to do it. For this picture I have to do it three or four times."

*Right:* **Empire Theatre, London, October 29, 1956**
In a low-cut gown that ensured maximum press coverage, Marilyn is presented to Queen Elizabeth II at the Royal Film Performance of The Battle of the River Plate. Actor Victor Mature can be seen on Marilyn's right.

# ★ The Prince and the Showgirl

The frothy, romantic tale of a Ruritanian prince (played by Laurence Olivier), in London for the 1911 coronation, who gets involved with a beautiful chorus girl, Elsie Marina, played of course by Marilyn.

**Studio:** Warner Brothers
**Released:** June 1957
**Producer:** Laurence Olivier

**Director:** Laurence Olivier
**Format:** Technicolor
**Leads:** Laurence Olivier, Marilyn Monroe, Dame Sybil Thorndike

*Above:* **On set, 1956**

Sir Laurence Olivier directing Marilyn, with the actor Richard Wattis in the center background. Olivier later said of her: "She was the complete victim of ballyhoo and sensation … and she was exploited beyond anyone's means."

# Stand-in for Marilyn

Born in Croydon, London, Una Pearl had worked in repertory theater and had walk-on roles in films including *An Alligator Named Daisy* and *The Silken Affair* when, in June 1956, she got a call from a casting agent that Jack Cardiff was casting for body-doubles for *The Prince and the Showgirl*. Despite being ten years younger and two inches shorter than Marilyn, Una was picked from around 50 other girls, partly because she had exactly the same skin color.

She took to Marilyn as soon as they met on the film set:

**I found her charming, a giggler—the least little thing would set her off laughing. And she was very down to earth. I didn't find her snooty like some actresses, who wouldn't smile, and would look the other way if you said good morning.**

When the film was completed, Una appeared in three scenes of the final edit. Her long-fingered hands can be seen in close-up when Elsie Marina (Marilyn) reads a program booklet, and she also appears in long shot, waving to King George V in the coronation scenes. And when Marilyn was indisposed for medical reasons, Una was filmed from behind, curtsying to the Prince (Laurence Olivier).

A couple of years later, Una Pearl got the job as stand-in for Brigitte Bardot in *Babette Goes To War*—not bad for an "unknown" actress, being picked to double for the two most celebrated sex symbols of the 1950s.

*Above:* **Una Pearl, July 1956**
The British stand-in for Marilyn being interviewed by a reporter on what it was like to double for the most glamorous actress in the world.

*Next page:* **Publicity shot, 1956**
A seductive pose for the eminent photographer Richard Avedon, used as publicity for *The Prince and the Showgirl*.

*Above and left:* **The Prince and the Showgirl publicity, 1956**
Another publicity shot (left) for the release of *The Prince and the Showgirl,* by
Richard Avedon. The photographer is seen above talking to Marilyn
during the shoot.

She gave more to the still camera than any
actress ... any woman ... I've ever
photographed, infinitely more patient, more
demanding of herself and more comfortable in
front of the camera than away from it.

**Richard Avedon**

TECHNICOLOR®

*Above:* **Poster, The Prince and the Showgirl, June 1957**

*Left:* **Radio City, New York, June 13, 1957**
Arthur Miller and Marilyn arriving for the premiere of *The Prince and the Showgirl* at the Radio City Music Hall, New York.

# Sam Shaw, on set and off

At the beginning of the fifties, New York photographer Sam Shaw was working in Los Angeles, and was often commissioned by 20th Century Fox to design advertisements for their releases and take still photographs on the actual set.

It was around this period, 1950–51, that he got to know Marilyn. The star-to-be had still to break into the big time; indeed, at one point during an out-of-work period between assignments she became Sam's chauffeur just to pay the rent.

They became good friends, on and off the set, and when Fox started planning the making of *The Seven Year Itch*, Marilyn's agent at the time, producer Charles Feldman, hired Sam to document the actual making of the movie.

So it was that Sam Shaw was responsible for the idea of the open shoot on the streets of New York for the famous billowing skirt scene; most of the pictures one sees of that shoot—and the subsequent set-up in Hollywood of the same scene—were taken by Sam. Including, of course, the most familiar image that was used on posters and billboards the world over.

When Marilyn moved to New York in the mid-fifties, she often socialized with Shaw and his wife, and it was they who introduced her to Norman and Hedda Rosten who became lifelong friends, Hedda acting as Marilyn's personal secretary for a time.

And it was Sam—after visiting Marilyn in the hospital in the summer of 1957—who suggested to her husband Arthur Miller that

*Left:* **Sam Shaw on set with Marilyn, 1955**
As an on-set still photographer for Fox, Sam Shaw had known, and worked with, Marilyn since she had played bit parts in the very early fifties.

his short story *The Misfits* would make an ideal full-length feature film specifically to highlight Marilyn's talents as a dramatic actress. It was to be the first time Miller was to write a screenplay, having previously turned down all such suggestions.

Among the most personal off-set pictures that Shaw took of Marilyn were a series of images in and around New York City. Many were with Arthur Miller—in a boat on Central Park, under the Brooklyn Bridge, eating hot dogs, shopping on Fifth Avenue—evoking a tranquil period in a far-from-tranquil life.

Most of these intimate pictures were stocked away, gathering dust in cardboard boxes in New York, until Sam's son Larry discovered them after the photographer's death in 1999, eventually releasing them in book form via a German publisher.

Everybody knows about her insecurities, but not everybody knows what fun she was, that she never complained about the ordinary things in life, that she never had a bad word to say about anyone, and that she had a wonderful spontaneous sense of humor.

**Sam Shaw on Marilyn**

*Right:* **Dressing room, 1957**
Shaw caught Marilyn in this dressing-room shot putting finishing touches to her make-up.

*Above:* **New York City, fall 1956**

Photographer Sam Shaw chronicled Marilyn and Arthur Miller's life in New York in the fall of 1956 with a series of pictures evocative of the city and their part in it. He said of Marilyn's attachment to the city, "Brooklyn became Nirvana to her, a magical place, her true home."

*Above:* **Fifth Avenue, New York, fall 1956**
Here, Sam Shaw captures Marilyn—with onlooking spectators in the
background, of course—doing what every woman does on Fifth Avenue,
shopping for clothes.

With the possible exception of Colette's Cheri and a
few short stories ... I had not known her read
anything all the way through. There was no need
to: she thought she could get the idea of a book ...
in a few pages ... With no cultural pretentions to
maintain, she felt no need to bother with anything
that did not sweep her away.

**Arthur Miller**

*Left:* **Roxbury, Connecticut, 1957**
When Sam Shaw photographed Marilyn and Arthur Miller at their home
in Roxbury, Connecticut, he recorded an almost idyllic side to their
domestic life. Marilyn looked radiant and happy as she played and pouted
in front of the camera with her husband.

He's a brilliant man and a wonderful writer,
but I think he's a better writer than a husband.

Sam Shaw took pictures of Marilyn in the Miller summer home in the
Hamptons, Long Island.

With fame, you know, you can read about yourself, somebody else's ideas about you, but what's important is how you feel about yourself—for survival and living day to day with what comes up.

*Right:* **Idlewild Airport, NYC, July 17, 1957**

With Arthur Miller hovering in the background, a windswept Marilyn is besieged by reporters at New York's Idlewild Airport after her arrival from a vacation with her husband in Jamaica. The main reason for the journalists' interest were the rumors circulating at the time of Marilyn's possible pregnancy. "I have nothing to say," came from Marilyn, while Miller proved equally tight-lipped with "Not a word" when quizzed.

Her beauty and humanity shine through ...
she is the kind of artist one does not come on
every day in the week. After all, she was
created something extraordinary.

**Arthur Miller**

*Left:* **The Waldorf Astoria, New York, January 28, 1958**
The March of Dimes is a major American children's charity, founded by
President Roosevelt in 1938. Marilyn poses for photographs with the
"March of Dimes poster twins," six-year-old Lindy and Sandy Sue
Solomon, at the annual March of Dimes fashion show held in the Waldorf-
Astoria hotel in 1958. Wearing a champagne-colored satin dinner costume
designed by John Moore for Talmack, Marilyn introduced the show which
featured fashions by members of the couture group of the New York Dress
Institute and other designers from New York, California, and Italy.

## chapter 5

# Triumph and tragedy

# "A lost child" 1958–62

From early on it was clear that *Some Like It Hot* was going to be a minefield for director Billy Wilder, but even he—despite knowing, after *The Seven Year Itch* how difficult Marilyn could be to work with—didn't anticipate just how fraught the production was going to be.

To start with, Marilyn objected to the film being shot in black and white rather than color. She was angry that the studio cast Jack Lemmon in a role originally earmarked for Frank Sinatra. Although these early issues were ironed out, she hated working with Tony Curtis (the feeling was mutual); her working style also got more and more frustrating for Wilder—and her fellow actors—as the shooting progressed through August, September, and October of 1958.

Even when she was there in front of the camera, she would demand take after take—her mentors Lee and Paula Strasberg had taught her to do a shot again and again until she felt she had it right. Sequences that should have taken an hour to complete took days, the budget was spiralling out of control, and Wilder was on the point of despair: "She was impossible, not just difficult."

Her mood changes and late appearances—she would often turn up in the early evening for a shoot scheduled to start at noon—were certainly related to her deteriorating mental stability, and after six weeks on the film she was admitted to the Cedars of Lebanon Hospital for "nervous exhaustion."

Despite everything, the filming work on *Some Like It Hot* was finished at the beginning of November, and it opened in March 1959. It became one of the best-loved and commercially successful film comedies of all time—and certainly the most successful film in Marilyn's career.

Meanwhile, Marilyn, who was in the early stages of another

pregnancy while still shooting the movie, miscarried again in mid-December 1958. It was to be the last time that she would try for a baby. An increasing reliance on sleeping tablets and other barbiturates in the months following was to characterize the rest of her life.

While Marilyn had been filming *Some Like It Hot*, Arthur Miller was putting in place *The Misfits*, for which he had secured John Huston as prospective director. There was a part specifically written for Marilyn, and Miller's idea was to have Clark Gable play the other lead role. He would not finally secure Gable's signature until January 1960, by which time Marilyn was set to embark on another film in the interim—a comedy directed by George Cukor, *Let's Make Love*.

The lead role in the new film went to the French actor Yves Montand—after being turned down by Gregory Peck, Cary Grant, Rock Hudson, and Charlton Heston, and shooting began in the first few weeks of 1960. Montand arrived from San Francisco (where he'd been performing in a one-man stage show) with his wife, actress Simone Signoret. They moved into a bungalow next to where Marilyn and Arthur Miller were staying, at the Beverly Hills Hotel. Very soon the two couples—who were already acquainted, Arthur having known the Montands since 1956—were a regular social foursome.

The Miller/Monroe marriage had been hitting increasingly bad patches over the preceding months, and the camaraderie of the four of them with Marilyn and Yves also in a working relationship could have been an ideal scenario for marital reconciliation—or, as it turned out, final disintegration.

In April, Marilyn and Yves found themselves without their partners in Hollywood; Simone Signoret had returned to Europe for a new film assignment, and Arthur Miller was in the Nevada desert with John Huston looking at locations for the upcoming *Misfits*. The two stars of *Let's Make Love* did just that, as they embarked on an affair that would carry on through the rest of the film's shooting.

In many ways *Let's Make Love* was a curious project, a quirky show-biz-based musical comedy which featured Tony Randall and British pop singer Frankie Vaughan, and Marilyn was full of doubts about it right throughout production—doubts, of course, which surfaced as misgivings about her own ability. Her doubts were misplaced inasmuch as she gave a convincing performance, along with one of the truly memorable production numbers of her career as she sang "My Heart Belongs To Daddy" clad in a black leotard.

Reassurance about her own talent—and reassurance was something Marilyn was increasingly in need of—came in March when she received a Golden Globe Award from the Foreign Press Association as "Best Actress in a Comedy or Musical" for her role in *Some Like It Hot.*

The filming for *The Misfits* began in the desert around Reno, Nevada, on July 18, 1960. The almost lunar landscapes gave a stark edge to the drama centered on a latter-day cowboy played by Gable, Marilyn's divorcee who falls for him, and a disillusioned rodeo rider, Montgomery Clift. Shooting on Marilyn's scenes was interrupted at the end of August when she was flown to Westside Hospital, Los Angeles, having suffered a nervous breakdown. She was back on the set ten days later.

As shooting finished in November it was announced to the press that Marilyn's marriage to Arthur Miller was to be dissolved.

After her divorce from Miller was granted in January 1961, Marilyn suffered more frequent lapses in her health brought on by her increasing dependence on both medication and alcohol, occasioning more visits to psychiatric and medical clinics.

Despite being out of the studios for the entire year, she was dogged by journalists and photographers as never before, most of whom were more interested in her private life than her professional one.

One person who was seen to support her in increasingly difficult circumstances was Joe DiMaggio, who had remained a friend throughout the years since their marriage. Towards the end of 1961, rumors began to circulate of Marilyn having sexual affairs with both the President, John F. Kennedy and his brother Robert, the Attorney General, having been introduced to them by their brother-in-law, actor Peter Lawford.

Affairs notwithstanding, her friendship with the Kennedys was confirmed for the world to see on May 19, 1962, when Marilyn appeared at JFK's birthday celebration in Madison Square Garden, singing "Happy Birthday, Mr President" in front of 15,000 Democrats.

A month earlier, shooting had started on *Something's Got To Give*, a romantic comedy directed by George Cukor and also starring Dean Martin, Cyd Charisse, and Phil Silvers. Marilyn's unreliability—not just being late, but sometimes not showing up at all—eventually prompted Fox to fire her, suing her for half-a-million dollars for the cancellation of the film.

Although the studio eventually climbed down, preparing to negotiate with Marilyn about her work still to be done on the film, it was never to be. On the morning of August 5, 1962, she was found dead in the bedroom of her house in the Brentwood suburb of Los Angeles, allegedly clutching a telephone in one hand and a bottle of sleeping pills in the other. Controversy and conspiracy theory surrounded the case, and still does so today.

But, whatever the cause and circumstance of the tragedy, a star had died, and a legend was born.

I think Marilyn was as mad as a hatter.

**Tony Curtis**

## ★ Some Like It Hot

A sharp, fast-moving comedy in which Curtis and Lemmon, disguised as girls in an all-female band to escape the Mob, are faced with the undoubted charms of singer Sugar Kane Kowalczyk.

Studio: **United Artists**
Released: **March 1959**
Producer: **Billy Wilder**

Director: **Billy Wilder**
Format: **Monochrome**
Leads: **Tony Curtis, Jack Lemmon, Marilyn Monroe**

*Previous page:* **Some Like It Hot, September 1958**

A still from what is undoubtedly Marilyn Monroe's most celebrated movie, *Some Like It Hot*, with the co-star who probably least liked working with her, Tony Curtis.

*Right:* **Some Like It Hot, August 1958**

Sugar Kane's entrance scene. It included the famous "Jello" line, where Marilyn walks down the platform, as only she could, with Curtis and Lemmon's "Josephine" and "Daphne" standing in awe.

# It's like Jello on springs!

**Jack Lemmon to Tony Curtis in Some Like It Hot**

305

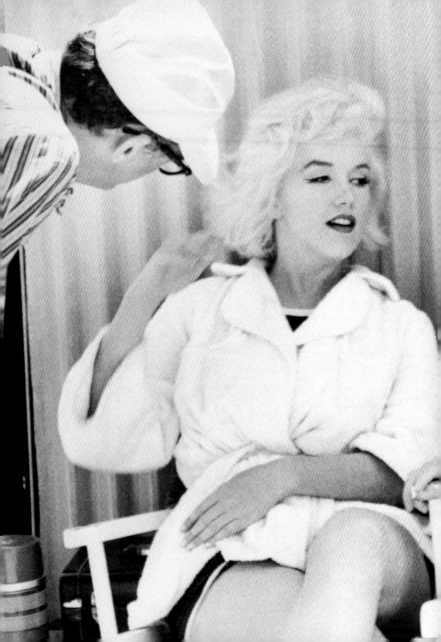

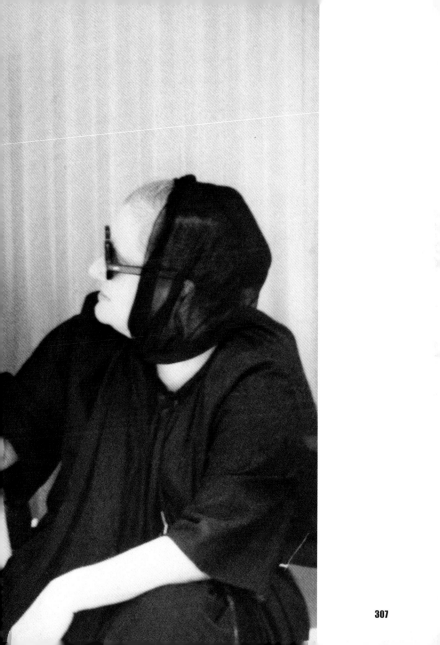

*Previous page:* **Hotel del Coronado, September 1958**

The location shooting on *Some Like It Hot* took place in the Victorian-inspired Hotel del Coronado outside San Diego, and on the beach in front. Here Arthur Miller talks to Marilyn and Paula Strasberg, between takes.

*Left:* **Some Like It Hot, August 1958**

Marilyn looking seductive in the railroad sleeper sequence. Making the film became a trial of patience for director Wilder and the rest of the cast and crew, as her apparent inability to get lines right seemed to be at an all-time peak; a situation that was made no better by the constant presence of Paula Strasberg, acting as her personal dialogue coach.

It used to be you'd call her at 9 am, she'd show up at noon. Now you call in May, she shows up in October.

**Billy Wilder**

# Kissing Marilyn Monroe was like kissing Hitler.

**Tony Curtis**

*Left:* **Some Like It Hot, November 1958**
Tony Curtis taking it like a man. Despite his famous description of what it was like kissing Marilyn, the movie elicited one of the classic performances of his long career. With many of the scenes involving them wearing drag, the long waits for Marilyn to get things right were often literally painful for Curtis and Jack Lemmon, both standing around in their high heels.

*Right:* **Maurice Chevalier, Hollywood, November 1958**
French singing star and actor Maurice Chevalier visited Marilyn during the final shoots for *Some Like It Hot*. Here, she wears a gown from the film designed by Orry-Kelly, who won an Oscar for the movie's costumes.

# She has a certain indefinable magic that comes across, which no other actress in the business has.

**Billy Wilder**

*Left:* **Loew's Capitol Theater, New York, March 29, 1959**
Marilyn speaks to radio announcer Ted Brown as she arrives for the premier of *Some Like It Hot* on New York's Broadway. During interviews out front before the premier she sounded uncertain about the film's reception, having not seen the whole film up until then. But when she saw it that evening, she was delighted. It has since been judged her greatest movie, and at the time garnered the best reviews that she was to receive of any throughout her career.

**Marilyn does herself proud, giving a performance of such intrinsic quality that you begin to believe that she's only being herself...**

**New York Post**

*Previous page:* **New York, February 5, 1959**
Author Carson McCullers greets Marilyn at a luncheon at her home in honor of the Danish author Karen Blixen (Isak Dinisen), on the right.

*Left:* **New York, May 13, 1959**
Dr Filippo Donini, Director of the Italian Cultural Institute, presenting Marilyn with Italy's coveted David di Donatello Award as best Foreign Actress of 1958, which she won for *The Prince and the Showgirl*. Also in the picture is Italian actress Anna Magnani, who won the Oscar for Best Actress in 1955 for her role in *The Rose Tattoo*.

*Right:* **Lennox Hill Hospital, June 26, 1959**

Marilyn is accompanied by Arthur Miller leaving the Lennox Hill Hospital on East 77th Street, New York, where she had been admitted to undergo gynaecological surgery for endometriosis four days earlier.

**She's scared and unsure of herself. I found myself wishing that I were a psychoanalyst and she were my patient. It might be that I couldn't have helped her, but she would have looked lovely on a couch.**

**Billy Wilder**

##  Let's Make Love

Musical showbiz comedy with Marilyn as the off-Broadway actress aspiring to better things.

**Studio:** 20th Century Fox
**Released:** September 1960
**Producer:** Jerry Wald

**Director:** George Cukor
**Format:** Cinemascope and color by DeLuxe
**Leads:** Marilyn Monroe, Yves Montand

# Interview with Bob Willoughby

PHOTOGRAPHER        Vence, France, February 17, 2004

**Photographer Bob Willoughby took a sensational series of pictures of Marilyn on the set of Let's Make Love, including the one on the right.**

"I was doing the shoot for *American Weekly* which was a national supplement that went in all the Hearst newspapers. It was for an article called 'Marilyn's Men,' and I was there with the writer. There were other photographers there of course, and 'Marilyn's men'—the director George Cukor, actors Yves Montand and Tony Randall, and Arthur Miller. Marilyn was wearing a leotard. The shots were done on the actual stage that was in the movie, and I think the picture tells more about what I feel about Marilyn than any other I did. The idea of a lost child, the vulnerability, it says all that. She's the lost child."

*Previous pages left and right:* **In rehearsal, Let's Make Love, January 1960** Marilyn rehearses a number with choreographer Jack Cole, who had previously worked with her on all her dance routines for *Gentlemen Prefer Blondes*, *River of No Return* and *There's No Business Like Show Business*.

CINEMASCOPE     COLOR by DE LUXE

GEORGE CUKOR     NORMAN KRASNA     HAL KANTER

If Marilyn is in love with my husband, it proves she has good taste. I am in love with him too.

**Simone Signoret**

*Above:* **Hollywood, June 1, 1960**

Director George Cukor (left) helps Marilyn with a pearl necklace given to her for her thirty-second birthday by the cast and crew of *Let's Make Love*, while co-star Yves Montand—with whom Marilyn embarked on an affair—looks on.

*Above left:* **Hollywood, early 1960**

Simone Signoret with husband Yves Montand (to her left), Marilyn with Arthur Miller, at dinner in Hollywood following their press conference announcing the forthcoming shooting of *Let's Make Love*.

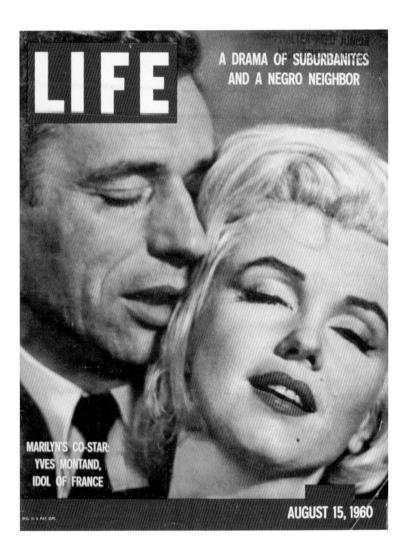

LIFE

A DRAMA OF SUBURBANITES
AND A NEGRO NEIGHBOR

MARILYN'S CO-STAR:
YVES MONTAND,
IDOL OF FRANCE

AUGUST 15, 1960

REG. U.S. PAT. OFF.

# I bent over to kiss her goodnight, but suddenly it was a wild kiss, a fire, a hurricane. I couldn't stop.

**Yves Montand**

*Left:* **Life magazine, August 15, 1960**

The press were agog at the far-from-private affair between Montand and and Marilyn, who toasted her French co-star at the launch of the movie with the words: "Next to my husband and Marlon Brando, I think Yves Montand is the most attractive man I've ever met."

*Left:* **Cal-Neva Lodge, Lake Tahoe, Nevada, 1960**

Before their eventual break up, the Millers still enjoyed social occasions together. Her husband was sitting to her left as she and Frank Sinatra chatted to Wingy Grover, manager of the Cal-Neva Lodge, Lake Tahoe, Nevada, in 1960. Sinatra owned the casino resort from 1960 to 1963, and Marilyn had a regular room there, chalet 52.

We are all born sexual creatures, thank God, but it's a pity so many people despise and crush this natural gift. Art, real art, comes from it—everything.

# MILLER WALKS OUT ON MARILYN

**Singling Herself Out.**

*Above and right:* **New York newspapers, November 1960**

Although Marilyn's separation from Arthur Miller was triggered in part by her six-month relationship with Yves Montand—the pair are seen enjoying a joke together on the front of the *New York Mirror*—it was not announced officially until after the affair had ended, at the completion of shooting of Marilyn's next film, *The Misfits*.

FINAL ★★ 5¢

**New York Mirror**

WEATHER: Fair and milder. Highest temperatures in the 50s.

SATURDAY, NOVEMBER 12, 1960          C

# MARILYN, MILLER
# ALL WASHED UP

STORY ON PAGE 3

## 4-Yr. Hitch Off

It's finis for the four-year "perfect marriage" of Marilyn Monroe and Arthur Miller (above). They were mutually bored, according to Hollywood correspondent Sheilah Graham, and would have broken up even if she hadn't met French film star Yves Montand, with whom she is chummy at recent party. She'll file for divorce.

[Other ____, Page 2; Center Fold]

335

 **The Misfits**

The disillusioned rodeo rider, ageing cowboy, and divorcee woman thrown together as they go catching mustangs in the harsh desert landscape around Reno, Nevada.

Studio: **United Artists**
Released: **February 1961**
Producer: **Frank E. Taylor**

Director: **John Huston**
Format: **Monochrome**
Leads: **Clark Gable, Marilyn Monroe, Montgomery Clift**

*Left:* **The Misfits on location, July 1960**

On location in Nevada at the start of shooting. Clockwise from the top: writer Arthur Miller, Eli Wallach (seated), director John Huston, Clark Gable, Marilyn Monroe, Montgomery Clift, and producer Frank E. Taylor.

She went right down into her own personal experience for everything, reached down and pulled something out of herself that was unique and extraordinary. She had no techniques. It was all the truth, it was only Marilyn. But it was Marilyn, plus. She found things, found things about womankind in herself.

John Huston

The shooting of *The Misfits* came at an increasingly troubled time in Marilyn's life. As well as her affair with Yves Montand coming to an end during the latter stages of the summer-long location work, on August 26, 1960, she suffered a nervous breakdown and had to be flown to Westside Hospital, Los Angeles. The pressures brought to bear during the filming were seen as being partly to blame, but although her own doctor, Hyman Engelberg, officially put it down to "exhaustion," there was much speculation that a failed suicide attempt had prompted her internment. During a ten-day stay in the hospital she was visited by Marlon Brando, Frank Sinatra, and ever-caring Joe DiMaggio, before returning to Nevada to resume filming.

*Above:* **Huston, Monroe, Miller, summer 1960**

Despite the apparent camaraderie in the on-set photographs, the making
of *The Misfits* was fraught with problems, from director John Huston's
budget-busting spending on the film, to Marilyn's absence through illness
and Arthur Miller's constant re-writes of the screenplay.

*Left:* **With Montgomery Clift, July 1960**

Of all Marilyn's co-stars through her career, Montgomery Clift was the most ebullient in his praise of her acting. A fellow alumnus of the Actors' Studio, in *The Misfits* he played the itinerant, disillusioned rodeo rider Perce Howland. Like Marilyn's Roslyn, he finds the roping of wild "misfit" mustangs cruel and mercenary, the two human misfits attempting to free the horses against the wishes of their captor, played by Clark Gable.

She listens, wants, cares. I catch her laughing across a room and I bust up. Every pore of that lovely translucent skin is alive, open every moment—even though this world could make her vulnerable to being hurt. I would rather work with her than any other actress. I adore her.

**Montgomery Clift**

I like her but she's so damn unprofessional …
she didn't show up 'till after lunch some days,
and then she would blow take after take …
I'm glad this picture's finished, she damn near
gave me a heart attack.

**Clark Gable**

*Right:* **Look magazine, January 1961**

Less than two weeks after production on *The Misfits* was completed, on November 16, 1960, Marilyn's co-star and lifetime screen idol Clark Gable died of a heart attack. Although the Hollywood legend found Marilyn difficult to work with—his assertion that she could have given him heart failure being particularly ironic—he had nothing but praise for her in other respects: "Marilyn is completely feminine, without guile … with a million sides to her."

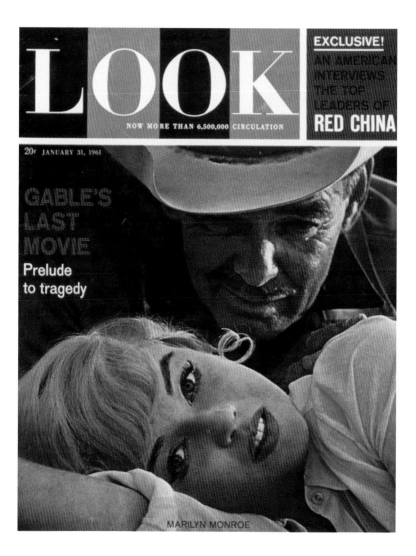

# LOOK

NOW MORE THAN 6,500,000 CIRCULATION

20¢   JANUARY 31, 1961

GABLE'S
LAST
MOVIE
Prelude
to tragedy

MARILYN MONROE

343

Marilyn is a kind of ultimate. She is uniquely feminine. Everything she does is different, strange, and exciting, from the way she talks to the way she uses that magnificent torso. She makes a man proud to be a man.

**Clark Gable**

*Left:* **Reno, Nevada, summer 1960**

Marilyn in her hotel room in Reno, Nevada during the location shooting of *The Misfits*. When it was released in February 1961 the movie was greeted by mixed reviews. *Variety* described it as "… a complex mass of introspective conflicts, symbolic parallels and motivational contradictions, the nuances of which may seriously confound general audiences," while some, such as the New York *Herald Tribune*'s Paul V. Beckley, were more positive: "The Misfits is so distinctly American nobody but an American could have made it. To be honest, I'm not sure anybody could have made it except John Huston from an original script by Arthur Miller, and it is hard to believe Miller could have written it without Marilyn Monroe."

# Shadows

There was a shadow that hung over Marilyn throughout her life. Since the star's childhood, her mother Gladys had been in psychiatric institutions of one kind or another, and was to remain in clinics and "rest homes" until her death in 1984, apparently hardly recalling Norma Jeane, and with no notion that her daughter had become Marilyn Monroe.

Marilyn's own emotional stability was always clouded by this knowledge, and from early in 1955 she had regularly consulted a psychotherapist—first of all Margaret Hohenberg, who had been treating Milton Greene for some years, and, from 1957, Marianne Kris. Vienna-born Kris was steeped in Freudian psychoanalysis; indeed, she underwent analysis by Sigmund Freud himself, and she and her husband Ernst Kris fled the Nazis with the Freud family in 1938, Freud calling her his "adopted daughter."

This therapy, that involved delving into her own childhood (aspects of which she had sublimated into her subconscious) arguably aggravated rather than remedied Marilyn's lack of self-confidence. Over the five years that she visited Dr. Kriss's consulting room her mood swings became more extreme, and her fits of depression more frequent—all being cushioned, of course, by "medication" (some of which was prescribed by Kris), and, to a lesser extent, alcohol.

In August 1957, the first of two miscarriages plunged Marilyn into her deepest emotional crisis yet, followed by an attempted suicide. Over the next year things got worse, and, in September 1958, she was admitted to the Cedars of Lebanon Hospital for what was described as "nervous exhaustion," followed at the end of the year by a second miscarriage.

Dear Lee and Paula,

Dr. Kris has had me put into the New York Hospital - psichiatric division under the care of two idiot doctors - they both should not be my doctors.

You haven't heard from me because I'm locked up with all these poor nutty people. I'm sure to end up a nut if I stay in this nightmare - please help me Lee, this is the last place I should be - maybe if you called Dr. Kris and assured her of my sensitivity and that I must get back to class so I'll be better prepared for "Rain".

And the science memories around here I'd like to forget - like screaming women etc.

Please help me - if Dr. Kris assures you I am all right - you can assure her I am not. I do not belong here!

I love you both,
Marilyn

P.S. forgive the spelling - and theres nothing to write on here. I'm on the dangerous floor its like a cell. Can you imagine - cement blocks. they put me in here because they lied to me about calling my doctor and Joe and they had the bathroom door locked so I broke the glass and outside of that I haven't done anything that is uncooperative.

Lee, I try to remember what you said once in class "that art goes far beyond science"

The gradual disintegration of her marriage to Arthur Miller did not help things, and in the middle of shooting *The Misfits*, in August 1960, Marilyn suffered a nervous breakdown, being briefly hospitalized at the Westside Hospital in Los Angeles. All those around her who cared for her well-being agreed that her problems were exacerbated by an increasing dependence on barbiturates, in the main prescribed by two of her doctors, Ralph Greenson and Hyman Engelberg.

Although she now consulted psychoanalyst Greenson when she was on the West Coast, Marilyn still visited Marianne Kris when in New York City. And it was Dr. Kris, perhaps unwittingly, who was to arrange for the most nightmarish hospital confinement of the increasingly disturbed star's life.

With her marriage to Arthur Miller finally dissolved (the divorce finalized at the end of January 1961) and the less than rapturous reception accorded her last two movies, *Let's Make Love* and *The Misfits*, Marilyn descended into an inconsolable depression at the beginning of February.

Considering her patient potentially suicidal, Kris suggested she check herself in to the New York Hospital, driving her there on Tuesday, February 7. Marilyn (using the name "Faye Miller" to avoid publicity) signed herself in to the Payne Whitney Clinic, which was the hospital's psychiatric division.

Although she knew the clinic dealt with psychiatric problems, what Marilyn didn't expect was to be treated as one of their disturbed patients, being incarcerated in what amounted to a cell—a small room with no telephone and the door locked, a pane in the door allowing passing staff to observe her. Over the next days, things got worse and after writing an emotional letter to the Strasbergs (reproduced on the previous page) begging for help, she was able to ring Joe DiMaggio in Florida, who came to her "rescue" immediately.

Amid a flurry of press speculation about her mental condition, Marilyn was checked out of the clinic by DiMaggio after four traumatic days—during which she had allegedly smashed the window on her door and tore off her hospital gown in fits of desperation. She spent the next three weeks in the comfortable surroundings of Columbia Presbyterian Medical Center.

It was the end of Marilyn's relationship with Marianne Kris, who she dismissed following her discharge from the Medical Center. And it was also the beginning of the loyal attention that Joe DiMaggio would pay his still-troubled ex-wife right up to the time of her tragic death, just eighteen months later.

There was no empathy at Payne Whitney—it had a very bad effect on me. They put me in a cell (I mean cement blocks and all) for very disturbed, depressed patients, except I felt I was in some kind of prison for a crime I hadn't committed.

*Previous page:* **Columbia Presbyterian Medical Center, New York, March 5, 1961**

Concluding nearly a month of psychiatric treatment, Marilyn leaves the Columbia Presbyterian Medical Center. Besieged by reporters and press photographers, she had to be escorted through a cordon of sixteen policemen and hospital security guards to her waiting limousine.

*Left:* **Polyclinic Hospital, New York, July 11, 1961**

Marilyn leaves the Polyclinic Hospital in Manhattan after undergoing a gall bladder operation, her fifth visit to the hospital in ten months. Again, she was virtually mobbed by well-wishers and journalists as she left.

*Right:* **Yankee Stadium, NYC, April 1961**

From the moment he "rescued" her from the psychiatric ward of the Payne Whitney Clinic, Joe DiMaggio returned to Marilyn's life in a consistently supportive role. As soon as she left the more preferable Presbyterian Medical Center at Columbia University, where Joe had her transferred, he took her to the New York Yankees training camp, then on to the Florida resort of Redington Beach. Here the couple are snapped watching a baseball game at DiMaggio's old home ground, the Yankee Stadium in the Bronx.

# It wasn't Hollywood that destroyed her—she was a victim of her friends.

**Joe DiMaggio**

She was getting out of relationships that were not good for her and back into one that was. She knew she needed some sort of emotional and spiritual anchor.

**Susan Strasberg**

*Left:* **Miami, February 21, 1962**
Joe DiMaggio and Marilyn exchange a farewell kiss as she leaves Miami, Florida, for a vacation in Mexico. Their seemingly platonic relationship at this point was, nevertheless, potentially more than that as her ex-husband often seemed to be the only solid support she could rely on in an increasingly troubled period of her life.

*Right:* **Golden Globe Awards, Hollywood, March 5, 1962**

Actor Rock Hudson (who had been approached, unsuccessfully, to play opposite Marilyn in both *Bus Stop* and *Let's Make Love*) presenting her with the 1961 "World Film Favorite" Golden Globe award from the Hollywood Foreign Press. Although never receiving an Academy Award, she had won the same accolade in 1954, and the 1959 Best Actress in a Comedy or Musical Golden Globe for her performance in *Some Like It Hot*.

# Fame is fickle and I know it. It has its compensations, but it also has its drawbacks and I've experienced them both.

*Right:* **Golden Globe Awards, Hollywood, March 5, 1962**

Marilyn attended the Golden Globe awards dinner in the company of José Bolanos, a screenwriter she had met while on vacation in Mexico, bringing him back to escort her to the ceremony. In a tight-fitting dress that had the flashbulbs popping, Marilyn was visibly intoxicated for most of the evening. The affair, if you could call it that, with José Bolanos was short lived. As soon as Joe DiMaggio reappeared in LA he departed, later claiming he and Marilyn were planning to wed; it seems he was Marilyn's biggest fan, who got nearer to his dream woman than he could have ever hoped to.

The fact is that the studios cannot operate with stars who do not report for work. If this sort of thing continues, there will be no movie industry at all.

**Henry Weinstein, producer**

## ★ Something's Got To Give

Due to Marilyn's suspension and subsequent death, the movie was never completed. It was later re-shot, with Doris Day, James Garner, and Polly Bergen playing the lead parts, as *Move Over Darling*.

Studio: 20th Century Fox

Producer: Henry T. Weinstein

Director: George Cukor

Leads: Marilyn Monroe, Dean Martin, Cyd Charisse

*Right:* **Something's Got To Give, May 1962**

It wasn't just Marilyn who caused delays in *Something's Got To Give*. The original production schedule had been put back from February to April because of numerous rewrites, so when Marilyn reported for shooting a week late because of illness, the film was already under pressure. More absence followed, including a flying trip to New York to attend the birthday bash for John F. Kennedy, and a financially embattled studio—probably looking for an excuse to pull the plug on the whole project—dismissed its biggest star amidst much acrimony, before cancelling the movie altogether.

# LIFE

**New Evidence That**
## CANCER MAY BE INFECTIOUS

**MARILYN MONROE**
A SKINNY-DIP
YOU'LL NEVER SEE
ON THE SCREEN

ALSO THIS WEEK
## THE MIGHTY U.S. NAVY
Its Fighting Men,
Its Global Power
18 Pages of Picture
Maps and Drawing

Latest Hairdo
the 'Marienbad'

**JUNE 22 · 1962 · 20¢**

*Left:* **Something's Got To Give, May 1962**

Although Fox reportedly shot over eight hours of film, when she was dismissed the studio claimed that only seven minutes of Marilyn Monroe's material was usable. Some of that appeared in a 1963 Fox documentary simply called *Marilyn*, while other outtakes, rushes, make-up tests, and such have become much sought-after collector's items. Certainly the most sensational sequence that was completed by Marilyn was the swimming pool scene, in which she spontaneously removed her flesh-coloured bikini for what became an unexpected nude skinny dip in front of the cameras.

# The Kennedy connection

The exact circumstances of Marilyn Monroe's relationship with the US President John F. Kennedy and his brother Robert, the Attorney General at the time, have never been precisely established for obvious reasons. Notwithstanding their seats of power at the head of the most powerful nation on earth, they would have had good reason to keep any affairs clandestine simply as married men with families.

John ("Jack") Kennedy was known to be a notorious womanizer nevertheless, despite his much-idealized marriage to Jacqueline Bouvier. Bobby on the other hand was much more the solid family man, his marriage seemingly unblemished by infidelity, yet it was he, rather than his brother the President, with whom Marilyn had the closest relationship.

The link that brought Marilyn into the Kennedy orbit was the Hollywood actor Peter Lawford, who was part of the much-publicized "Clan"—the social "gang" of male hell-raisers later celebrated as the "Rat Pack" that comprised Dean Martin, Sammy Davies Jr, Joey Bishop, and its informal head honcho, Frank Sinatra. Marilyn had long been good friends with Sinatra, and so, not unnaturally, got to know Lawford; but the latter was also part of a much bigger, and certainly more prestigious, clan—the Kennedys— by virtue of his marriage to the President's sister Pat Kennedy, whom Marilyn came to consider a close friend.

*Right:* **Madison Square Garden, May 19, 1962**
John F. Kennedy sits in the center of the front row, behind the presidential seal, as Marilyn faces the most prestigious live audience of her career at the fund-raising event for the Democratic presidential campaign.

Accounts differ as to exactly when Marilyn first met the Kennedy brothers; all agree, however, that she met Bobby before the President, and both at dinner parties at the Lawfords' beach home in Santa Monica in 1961. Again, biographers' versions of the exact events vary, with one locating Marilyn's only bedroom liaison with the President when they were house guests of the famous singer Bing Crosby, and another at the president's regular Manhattan bolt-hole the Carlyle Hotel, from where he was known to have conducted a multiplicity of short-lived affairs with beautiful women.

One thing seems certain, Marilyn had no illusions about a long-term relationship with John F. Kennedy. As Lee and Paula Strasberg's actress daughter Susan, a close confidante of Marilyn, told biographer Donald Spoto:

## Not in her worst nightmare would Marilyn have wanted to be with JFK on any permanent basis. It was okay for one night to sleep with a charismatic president—and she loved the secrecy and drama of it.

Initially the rumors that began to sweep Hollywood and the gossip columns of the yellow press centered on Marilyn's relationship with the elder Kennedy, Mr President. This was seemingly confirmed for those who wished to believe it when the star famously appeared at JFK's birthday bash at Madison Square Garden in front of 15,000 adulatory big spenders, who had paid from a hundred to a thousand dollars per ticket.

The event on May 19, 1962—a fundraiser for the Democratic Party—was hosted by Jack Benny and included appearances by Ella Fitzgerald, Harry Belafonte, Maria Callas, Henry Fonda, and Peggy Lee among others. Marilyn was late turning up—so what was new?—and the organizers repeatedly found themselves having to reschedule the show around her absence. This resulted in Peter Lawford, who was to introduce her, announcing "… here she is Mr President, the late Marilyn Monroe."

Slipping off an ermine jacket to reveal a clinging flesh-colored body-stocking of a dress that left little to the imagination, Marilyn proceeded, nervously at first, with a wispy voiced version of "Happy Birthday," followed by a singalong second chorus with the whole audience joining in. She concluded her spot with a "Thanks Mr. President" version of "Thanks For The Memory," after which JFK commented in his keynote speech:

## I can now retire from politics after having had "Happy Birthday" sung to me by such a sweet, wholesome girl as Marilyn Monroe.

Marilyn's involvement with Robert Kennedy had the hallmarks of being a far more intense and longer-lasting affair, though it never eventually developed as such. From the start, meeting her at a dinner party at the Lawfords', he was apparently entranced by her. Through the weeks following his brother's birthday concert, the Attorney General took more and more interest in Marilyn—as a person as well as physically—which in turn made their affair more significant to her than a mere sexual encounter.

Clearly—especially from the Washington perspective—they were getting a little too close. As surely as Bobby had encouraged and nurtured their relationship, by the late summer he was distancing himself, the Kennedy family closing ranks, and Marilyn's calls to his office more often than not fielded by his secretary. How much this contributed, along with the alcohol and medication, to her mental low in early August, one can only speculate.

Claims that Bobby Kennedy had visited her home at Brentwood the day before her death were refuted by the whole family. In the wake of the tragedy, FBI director J. Edgar Hoover (a staunch Republican and no lover of the Kennedys) demanded a complete account of the Attorney General's movements that weekend. Kennedy explained he had been with his wife Ethel and four of their children, visiting friends—who confirmed his story—in San Francisco.

What is clear is that their involvement with Marilyn Monroe turned into a no-win situation for the dynastic political clan. Had Robert Kennedy got more involved to the point where rumor became scandal, doubtless his brother's liaisons with the star would have also been more firmly confirmed, risking the future of the presidency itself. But with her apparent suicide surrounded by conjecture, the slightest hint of their involvement in her death could have had even more traumatic repercussions in the corridors of power around the Oval Office. All of which has provided ample "motive" for the numerous "cover-up" allegations and conspiracy theories that have proliferated in print and on the Internet ever since.

*Left:* **Madison Square Garden, May 19, 1962**
Taking an unofficial break from filming *Something's Got To Give*, Marilyn arrives, an hour late and rather inebriated, for the fund raiser-cum-birthday celebration, for which she paid the $1,000 admission price.

# ... it was just skin and beads—only I didn't see the beads!

**US Ambassador to the United Nations, Adlai Stevenson, describing Marilyn's dress**

*Right:* **Madison Square Garden, May 19, 1962**

Marilyn sings. One of her briefest public performances, but certainly one of the most famous, concluded with a six-foot cake with forty-five giant candles being carried on to the stage by two chefs. For her costume, Marilyn had worked closely with designer Jean-Louis, whose brief was to "make a dress that only Marilyn Monroe would dare to wear." The $12,000 garment glistened with hand-sewn rhinestones, and under the spotlights the silk appeared transparent, giving the illusion of Marilyn being naked.

# Death of a goddess

Which ever way one looked at it, Marilyn Monroe's life in the middle of 1962 was in turmoil. Fox had fired her from a film and were in the process of canceling her contract. Both the Kennedys with whom she'd been involved were now actively distancing themselves from her. She was depending on drink and drugs to get her through the day, the latter mainly prescribed as medication by her doctor Hyman Engelberg. And she was under increasing psychological pressure from her analyst, Ralph Greenson.

From the viewpoint of many of those around Marilyn, Greenson was becoming a Svengali figure in her life. Even her housekeeper/nurse (though she declined to be referred to as either), Eunice Murray, who Greenson had hired, was making more and more decisions on behalf of Marilyn—often seemingly at the behest of the analyst. It was Mrs Murray rather than Marilyn who had found the house at Fifth Helena Drive, Brentwood, which Marilyn had moved into early in the year.

But there was a glimmer of light at the end of what otherwise appeared to be an ever-darkening tunnel. Joe DiMaggio had been a constant support over the previous year or so. They had spent Christmas 1961 together, and—notwithstanding the Kennedys and any other distractions—by mid-1962 were spending a lot more time in each other's company; Joe, if not Marilyn, hinting at the chance of a reconciliation.

At the same time Fox reversed their decision to cancel *Something's Got To Give*, opening negotiations with Marilyn to resume work on the picture. And, by the end of July, Marilyn had taken steps to replace Eunice Murray with her former housekeeper Florence Thomas, much to Ralph Greenson's chagrin, no doubt.

THE MONROE SAGA: 7 PAGES OF STORIES AND PICTURES

Friends concerned about Marilyn saw this as a step in the right direction, assuming Greenson would be next in line for dismissal.

But Marilyn's physical and mental state had taken a sudden turn for tho worse after she was admitted to the Cedars of Lebanon Hospital on July 20. According to a press person in her publicist's office, it was to have a pregnancy aborted, though this was never officially confirmed. By the end of the month she was in a deepening state of depression, and through Friday and Saturday, August 3 and 4, all who spoke to her confirmed that she seemed increasingly troubled. These included Peter Lawford, who was disturbed by her obviously slurred speech, and whose wife later claimed he was "haunted by her death."

*Right:* **Newspapers, August 6, 1962**
The impact of Marilyn's death reverberated around the world, evidenced by this selection of UK newspapers on the day after the news broke.

Unusually, Mrs. Murray stayed over on the Saturday night, and it was she who was to discover Marilyn's body in her locked bedroom in the early hours of Sunday. The housekeeper rang Greenson, who in turn alerted Engelberg (who just days before had prescribed a large quantity of Nembutal pills that were now, fatally, in her system), the latter pronouncing Marilyn Monroe dead. When the police arrived, they found a stack of Frank Sinatra discs still on the record player. The Certificate of Death gave the cause as "acute barbiturate poisoning, ingestion of overdose," adding "Probable Suicide."

After a brief interval at the coroner's morgue, Marilyn's body was moved to the Westwood Village Memorial Park mortuary, where three of her most loyal employees made her ready, as they had in life: Agnes Flanagan, her hairdresser, her costumier Margie Pilcher, and make-up artist Allan "Whitey" Snyder. Whitey carried a message from Marilyn engraved on a money clip, a gift from ten years earlier when she'd made him promise to do her make-up should anything happen to her. He'd joked that he'd do it if her body was still warm, and the message read "Whitey—While I'm still warm, Marilyn."

The funeral of Marilyn Monroe, at the insistence of a heart-broken Joe DiMaggio, was only attended by thirty people—family and friends, with no Hollywood stars, studio people or reporters present. They included the Strasbergs, the Greensons, Eunice Murray, and Marilyn's half-sister Bernice. Only after the ceremony was over were the public and the world's press allowed near the marble-walled crypt where her coffin lay.

Almost as soon as the cemetery gates were closed that night, Marilyn's death—like her life—had become grist for the rumor mill. The star's relationship with the Kennedys, even if it in fact ran to just the most casual of liaisons, triggered conspiracy theories rivaled only by those thrown up in the wake of the brothers' own deaths.

# Marilyn Kills Self

## Found Nude In Bed ...
## Hand on Phone ...
## Took 50 Sleep Pills

Stories on Pages 2, 3. Photos on Pages 2, 3 and Center Fold

### Begin Her Tempestuous Life Story on Page 3

Most tragic of all, the time, effort, and obsession that has gone into explaining Marilyn's death has done little to explain her life.

Gloria Steinem

*Left:* **Eunice Murray, November 1962**
Housekeeper and nurse Eunice Murray, whom Marilyn was planning to replace. She found the star dead in her bedroom on August 5, 1962.

# Rumor, cover-up or conspiracy?

A trickle of gossip and rumor regarding Robert Kennedy's part in events surrounding Marilyn's death soon became an avalanche. These ranged from the quite possible (though unproveable) suggestion that his "cooling" down of their affair directly contributed to her suicide, to more sensational scenarios that linked him to a possible homicide carried out by persons unknown. One such theory proposed that Kennedy had actually visited Marilyn's home on the afternoon prior to her death.

While ninety-nine percent of all these versions of events can be discounted as blatant profiteering or mere mischief-making, the FBI files (released after the 1975 amendment to the 1967 Freedom of Information Act) make interesting reading. The Kennedy file in the Justice Department (of which he was head) put an official stamp on his description of his movements that weekend: he was in San Francisco with his family. The document from the FBI—which clearly had its own agenda—is worth quoting at some length:

"The studio notified Marilyn that they were canceling her contract. This was right in the middle of a picture she was making. They decided to replace her with actress Lee Remick. Marilyn telephoned Robert Kennedy from her home at Brentwood, California, person-to-person, at the Department of Justice, Washington, D.C. to tell him the bad news. Robert Kennedy told her not to worry about the contract—he would take care of everything. When nothing was done, she again called him from her home to the Department of Justice, person-to-person, and on this occasion they had unpleasant words. She was reported to have threatened to make public their affair. On the day that

Marilyn died, Robert Kennedy was in town, and registered at the Beverly Hills Hotel."

More specific in the FBI documents is the assertion that Eunice Murray and Marilyn's secretary Pat Newcombe (who actually had little time for each other), were complicit in the star's suicide; a link was also made between Newcombe's subsequent "pay-off" and "left-wing" elements in Hollywood. Shades of Joe McCarthy!

"On the date of her death, March 4, 1962, her housekeeper put the bottle of pills on the night table. It is reported the housekeeper and Marilyn's personal secretary and press agent, Pat Newcombe, were cooperating in the plan to induce suicide. Pat Newcombe was rewarded for her cooperation by being put on the Federal payroll as top assistant to George Stevens Jr., head of the Motion Picture Activities Division of the US Information Service. His father, George Stevens Sr., is a left-wing Hollywood director, who is well known for specializing in the making of slanted and left-wing pictures."

Clearly various parties had their own interests to serve in the immediate aftermath of Marilyn's death. The political establishment represented by the Kennedys needed to distance themselves from events as much as possible, without appearing callous at the loss of someone they acknowledged publicly as a friend. Their political opponents, on the other hand, benefited from any smears directed at the First Family in the affair, and they could rely on the media to provide them. The fact that such conspiracy theories and revelations about her last days have proliferated rather than subsided over the years merely proves Marilyn's enduring status as a modern legend.

*Above:* **Westwood Park Chapel, Los Angeles, August 8, 1962**

Joe DiMaggio, seen here on the left of the cortege, flew in to look after the funeral arrangements, assisted by Marilyn's half-sister Bernice Miracle and business manager Inez Melson. The private service, which opened to the strains of Tchaikovsky's Sixth Symphony, was conducted by Reverend A.J. Soldan. It included, at Marilyn's request, Judy Garland's famous song *Over The Rainbow*, as well as biblical readings and a eulogy that was delivered by Lee Strasberg.

★★★★
FINAL

# DAILY ☐ NEWS

### NEW YORK'S PICTURE NEWSPAPER ®

5¢

Vol. 44, No. 37 *Copr. 1962 News Syndicate Co. Inc.* New York 17, N.Y., Tuesday, August 7, 1962* WEATHER: Cloudy, warm and humid

# DIMAG CLAIMS MARILYN'S BODY

## Joins Star's Sister; Rites Set

### Sought Herself —Then Death?

Of the many faces of Marilyn Monroe, this is perhaps the one with which her millions of admirers were best familiar. It reveals a pensive, introspective woman who was perhaps her own worst enemy. Another great enemy, according to director John Huston, was sleeplessness. As far back as 1960, he said, she was caught up in a "vicious circle" of sedatives and stimulants which, he felt, doomed her to death or an institution. Whatever the cause of her death, she is gone. Her second husband, Joe DiMaggio, who was to become one of her best friends, helped plan her funeral and burial arrangements. Last services will be held at the mortuary of Westwood Village Memorial Park; burial will follow in the adjoining cemetery, near two of her relatives.

*Stories on page 3; other pictures in centerfold*

# chapter 6
# Icon and legend

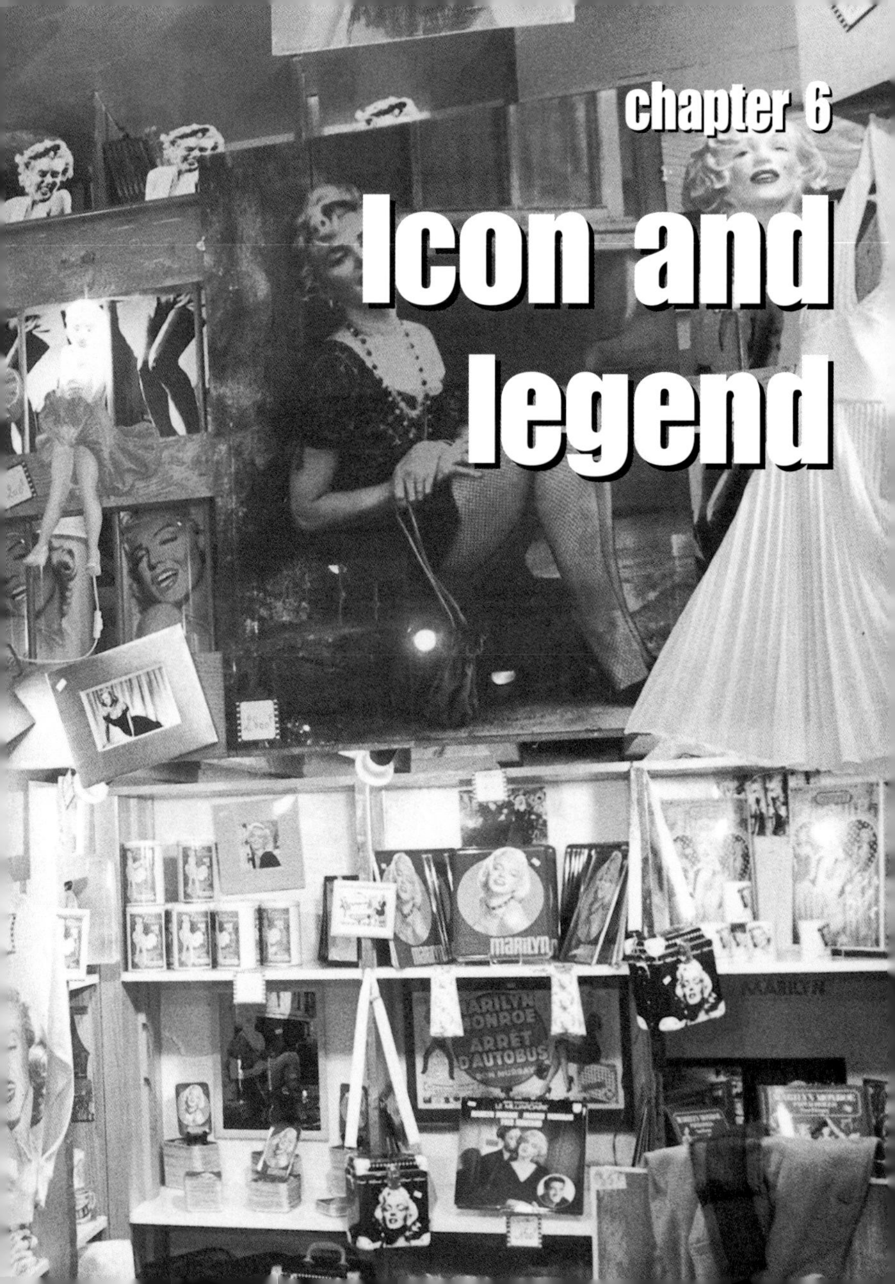

# "Last of the female superstars"

As well as the perhaps inevitable conspiracy theories, Marilyn's death also sparked a process that occurs just once or twice in a lifetime: the making of a true icon. Much of this was promulgated on the printed page. This ranged from the immediate magazine tributes to volume after volume of biography, much of which was about the writer rather than subject. The number of people who apparently had close affairs or other personal links with Monroe, enough to fill a book it would seem, grew along with the legend.

On the other hand, one of the most unusual—and critically well-received—evocations of the Monroe legend was the Nicholas Roeg film *Insignificance*, based on a 1982 London stage play by Terry Johnson. In the film, Marilyn, Albert Einstein, Senator Joseph McCarthy (played by Tony Curtis), and Joe DiMaggio (with Gary Busey as "The Ballplayer") meet in a New York hotel. Theresa Russell played "The Actress," none of the characters being named directly.

But the icon was more about image than the detail of her life—or fantasies based around it. This was to be expected with a star whose whole career was based on the notion of "look at me," whether on the front page of pin-up magazines, up there on the silver screen, or in front of a thousand star-struck onlookers on Hollywood Boulevard.

Her image became, like those of James Dean, Marlon Brando in his *Wild One* motorbike mode and the early Elvis, a symbol of the fifties and the innocent glamour it came to represent. In Marilyn's case, this was a glamour filtered through the sassy but vulnerable

*Right:* **Advertisement for video collection, 1992**
A 1992 video collection marking the 30th anniversary of Marilyn's last movie.

# 30 YEARS LATER, THE LEGEND LIVES ON!

In commemoration of the 30th anniversary
of Marilyn's last film, The Marilyn Collection
includes for the first time ever:

★ Original trailers
★ Collector cards of original theatrical art
★ *MovieTone News* footage of Marilyn

**7 ELEGANTLY REPACKAGED CLASSICS** $14⁹⁸ EACH **AND 5 NEW VIDEO RELEASES!**

USA
32

1995

characters of her film roles, and immortalized by photographers from the early on-the-road sessions with Andrés de Dienes to the nude "last sitting" with Bert Stern six weeks before her death.

The image soon became appropriated by popular culture generally, not just on postcards, posters and suchlike, but as a "design feature" on everything from T-shirts to tablemats, watches to wallpaper. She has even appeared on postage stamps in her home country and elsewhere—and, unlike most presidents and princes, is instantly recognizable. Marilyn soon became big in the "lookalike" industry, whether in glossy TV advertising or cheesy "greeting-grams" at parties. Others, like Madonna, simply took on aspects of the Monroe image as part of their own persona.

Even before her death, she was the subject of high art—or pop art, which was "high" art reflecting the "low" art of comics, movies, and advertising. Pop painters who featured her in their work included Peter Blake, Richard Hamilton, and Andy Warhol, whose silk-screen series of a 1952 photo itself became iconic.

More than forty years after her death, the legend lives on in those images that are in currency as much as ever. But the static iconography is not enough. Marilyn Monroe was a living, breathing, sexually driven, intellectually curious, emotionally fragile human being. To appreciate even a hint of what she was about we need to go back to the films, the core of her fame, and watch her move, listen to the songs, hear her—wide-eyed like a surprised child — breathlessly delivering her lines. The stereotype she unwittingly created has been part of the fabric of our culture ever since, but in those movies Marilyn was simply the original, the real thing.

*Left:* **USA commemorative postage stamp, 1995**
This stamp was the first in a Legends of Hollywood series.

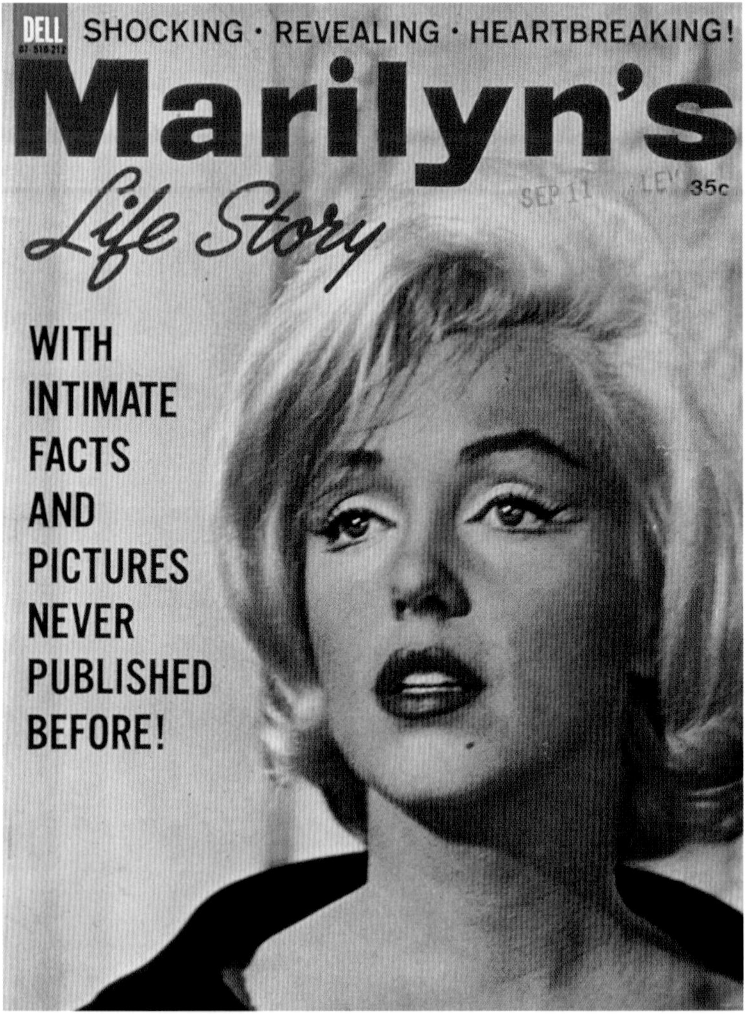
DELL
SHOCKING · REVEALING · HEARTBREAKING!
Marilyn's
Life Story
35c
WITH INTIMATE FACTS AND PICTURES NEVER PUBLISHED BEFORE!

She had such a magnetism that if fifteen men were in a room with her, each man would be convinced he was the one she'd be waiting for after the others left.

**Roy Craft, Marilyn's publicist**

*Left:* **Marilyn's Life Story, 1972**
The "shocking, revealing, heartbreaking" story of Marilyn was still able to shift pulp versions of her biography as if it had just happened, a full ten years after her death.

# The Monroe look

Long before her death, the Monroe image was aspired to by many of her contemporaries, mainly wannabe actresses hoping to impress the studios who were looking for the "next Marilyn." The hair, the figure, the walk, even the voice were aped to some degree or other by dozens of blonde bombshells, most of whom never got past the screen test.

Of those that did, Mamie Van Doren was among the most memorable, the buxom femme fatale of a dozen scorching B-movies including such teen-exploitation epics as *High School Confidential*, *Untamed Youth* and the marvelously titled *Sex Kittens Go To College*. Remembered, too, as almost a caricature Monroe, was Marilyn's nearest rival in the va-va-voom stakes—Jayne Mansfield—whose figure was literally over the top most of the time.

But, since her death, Marilyn's iconic status had been confirmed by more sincere homages, celebrating rather than imitating the original. In the 1970s, the New York band *Blondie* were named as such precisely because of lead singer Debbie Harry's image, one which she conceded was hugely influenced by Marilyn. In countless interviews, Harry has said that Marilyn was a major inspiration in how her "Blondie" persona was conceived. The first song she ever wrote was "Platinum Blonde" in which she pays homage to "Marilyn and Jean, Jayne, Mae, and Marlene," and her secret fantasy as a child was that Marilyn might possibly be her natural mother. "I always thought I was Marilyn Monroe's kid. I felt physically related and akin to her long before I knew she had been adopted herself. Of course, my continual participation in this maternal fantasy has changed drastically as I've grown up and discovered that quite a

few adopted girls have the same notion … She was the most controversial female while I was growing up, so she cast a large aura and I was very interested in that—her charisma."

Early in 1985, the chameleon-like Madonna put together what amounted to a tribute to Marilyn as the promotional video for her "Material Girl" single. In it, wearing a dress similar to the Billy Travilla classic, she performed a dance routine closely based on the "Diamonds Are A Girl's Best Friend" sequence from *Gentlemen*

*Above:* **Jayne Mansfield, c. 1956**
Often derided as a "poor man's Marilyn," the former Miss Photoflash 1952 is best remembered for her part in the 1956 rock'n'roll satire *The Girl Can't Help It,* which co-starred *Seven Year Itch* man Tom Ewell.

*Prefer Blondes*. It's a classic video and marked the beginning of the singer's obsession with film icons, particularly Monroe.

The singer went on to evoke the Marilyn legend more fully in a series of photographs for *Vanity Fair* magazine which deliberately reconstructed famous Monroe images, including pictures based on well-known photographs by Milton Greene, Marilyn on an elephant at Madison Square Garden, and the famous last nude sessions by Bert Stern. It caused controversy, with Madonna being accused of "body snatching Monroe," by Stern, who was so incensed by some of Madonna's photos that he contemplated legal action.

The latest high-profile example of someone adopting what the press described as a "Monroe look" was when the actress Scarlett Johansson appeared in a silver satin Prada dress and blonde hair-do à la Marilyn at the BAFTA ceremony in London, early in 2004—an effect repeated in a tight-fitting emerald number at the Oscars. Although the rising star looks little like the fifties screen goddess, just the association of a certain instantly recognizable "look" is enough for the media to make the link in the public mind—presumably just what Ms Johansson or her image-makers had in mind. Proving, once again, that Marilyn's visual persona has lost none of its potency more than fifty years after she first sashayed across cinema screens and magazine covers the world over.

*Above:* **Madonna, Hollywood, 1991**

Madonna performing her song "Sooner Or Later" at the 1991 Oscars
ceremony, in full Monroe style, in an outfit featured in the *Vanity Fair*
collection of Marilyn-inspired pictures by Steven Meisel.

# There will never be another like her, and Lord knows there have been plenty of imitators.

**Billy Wilder**

*Left:* **Kylie Minogue, 1999**
Australian singer Kylie Minogue did her own take on Marilyn's "Diamonds Are A Girl's Best Friend" routine at the opening of the Fox studios in Sydney, Australia, in 1999.

Our beloved Marilyn Monroe is still in the spirit world, and still studying philosophy, to make up for the education she never had as Norma Jeane Baker. Marilyn adored her public when she was alive, and that adoration remains the same today. She is eternally grateful that she is more of a legend on the other side than she was in life.

**Kenny Kingston, psychic**

*Right:* **Daily Mirror, February 17, 2004**
The British tabloid press were quick to draw the comparison with Marilyn Monroe when Scarlett Johansson adopted "the look" at the 2004 BAFTA and Oscar ceremonies.

*Next Page:* **Lookalikes, New York, 1993**
Actor Jason Priestley, known for his role in TV's *Beverly Hills 90210* (and who once said, "The great thing about Hollywood is there's always a bigger star than you"), with some Marilyn wannabes at a 1993 lookalike contest.

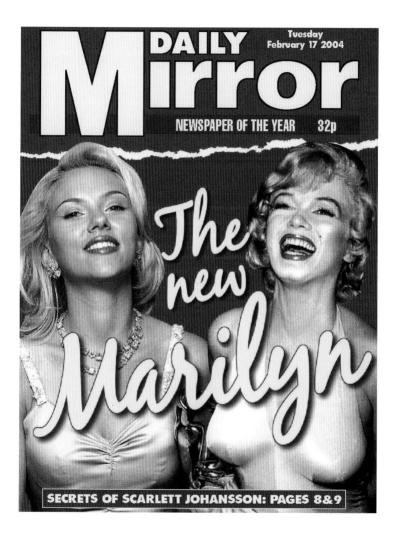

I suppose Monroe was just about the last of the female superstars to come out of the industry machine.

**Alexander Walker, film critic**

*Left:* **The Seven Year Itch doll, date unknown**

For every piece of vintage Marilyn memorabilia there are hundreds of items of merchandise on the market carrying the Monroe likeness, or at least purporting to. This *The Seven Year Itch* doll was part of a series.

*Left:* **Mural, Saltdean, Sussex, 2002**

Marilyn's image can be found in almost any context imaginable. This restaurant mural was painted in 2002 by Steven Smith as part of the restoration of the art deco-style Grand Ocean Hotel in Saltdean, Sussex, UK.

*Right:* **Wine bottle, California, 1980s**

In 1983, the California company Nova Wines negotiated an agreement with the Monroe Estate to carry her image and name on a range of wines. A royalty was directed, according to Marilyn's will, to Anna Strasberg to help support the Lee Strasberg Theater Institute, and to the Anna Freud Foundation in London, which set up a special child treatment center—the Monroe Young Family Center.

*Right:* **"Chanel No5," 1955**

Over the years, scores of advertisements in the press and on the screen have utilized the image of Marilyn using lookalike models. One that was genuinely authentic, however, was this 1990s advert for Chanel No5 perfume using a 1955 photograph taken by Ed Feingersh and incorporating Marilyn's famous reply to journalists when asked what she wore in bed.

# The secret of her delicious sexuality, admired as much by women as by men, was that it raised rather than devalued the female currency. It was as sweet, natural and over-flowing as a burst peach.

**Donald Zec, journalist**

'*What do I wear in bed? Why, Chanel No5, of course*'
Marilyn Monroe, 1952

*Above:* **Christie's, New York, October 1999**

In October 1999, an auction of personal property of Marilyn was held at Christie's New York. The white baby grand piano was bought by singer Mariah Carey for $662,500, on top of which can be seen the 1956 triptych photograph and eulogy to Marilyn by Cecil Beaton (presented to Marilyn by director Joshua Logan on the release of *Bus Stop*) which sold for $145,500.

*Above right:* **Christie's, New York, October 1999**

Telephone bids being received during the auction sale at Christie's, which realized $13.5 million benefiting various charities.

She had become a legend in her own time, and in her death took her place among the myths of our century.

**John Kobal, film historian**

*Above:* **Tommy Hilfiger, October 1999**

Fashion designer Tommy Hilfiger paid $42,550 at the Christie's auction for the denim jeans that Marilyn wore in *River Of No Return*, which he later displayed in one of his stores.

*Right:* **Canada, 1953**

Marilyn wears the same jeans while filming on location in Canada.

# Marilyn in art

Marilyn's image was rendered iconic in the purest sense of the word when she became the subject—even before her death—of "serious" visual art rather than just pinup portraits and publicity shots, skillful and artistic though many of these were in their own right. These included the work of renowned photographers, from Cecil Beaton to Bert Stern. But her image became an end in itself, a symbol rather than mere portraiture, when it began appearing in the rarefied environment of art galleries and museums as a "pop culture" cipher via the work of various painters, isolated from its more natural habitat of the world of the camera.

Artists who have committed Marilyn to canvas in this way have included such names as Willem de Kooning, Salvador Dali, Claes Oldenburg, and James Rosenquist, many of whom were exponents of the "pop art" that flourished in the sixties and later. But the artist who most successfully immortalized Marilyn in art, and who in many respects came to personify pop art, was the New York painter Andy Warhol. His embodiment of the pop art ethos in his work via the use of everyday objects and familiar images from popular culture—comics, movies, advertising—culminated in his adoption of silk-screen imagery to repeat his work, and variations of it, on an almost production-line basis. Indeed, his studio where he and his team created most of this work was known as The Factory.

Using photo-stencils in screen printing meant that Warhol could use photo images for his screen prints. The screen was prepared using a photographic process, with different color inks, then printed.

As it happened, Warhol began the silk-screen process around the time of Marilyn's death, in August 1962, and it was her image—from Frank Powolny's publicity shot for *Niagara*—that became the template for subsequent portraiture, with subjects as diverse as Elizabeth Taylor, Jackie Kennedy, and Chairman Mao Tse Tung.

In August 1962 I started doing silk screens. I wanted something stronger that gave more of an assembly line effect. With silk screening you pick a photograph, blow it up, transfer it in glue onto silk, and then roll ink across it so the ink goes through the silk but not through the glue. That way you get the same image, slightly different each time. It was all so simple, quick, and chancy. I was thrilled with it. When Marilyn Monroe happened to die that month, I got the idea to make screens of her beautiful face, the first Marilyns.

**Andy Warhol**

And despite their "mass production," original Warhol Marilyns have achieved the status of high art; in May 1998 a silk-screen print entitled "Orange Marilyn" was bought at auction by an anonymous buyer for $17.3 million, three times its expected price. But more importantly, by way of the mass dissemination of imagery that Warhol espoused throughout his work, his Marilyn has become possibly the most genuinely popular art image of modern times.

*Above:* **Andy Warhol, 1971**
Andy Warhol in front of his famous silk-screen portrait of Marilyn which he first created in 1962, based on the photograph opposite.

*Right:* **Publicity portrait, 1952**
The original photograph by Frank Powolny which was to be used as publicity for the film *Niagara*.

Marilyn actively wanted humanisation and emotionally she fought against becoming a symbol or an object ... Marilyn Monroe became a pair of lips, a walk, a set of numbers: 38–24–36.

**Paul Mayersberg**

*Right:* **Dress by Versace, 1990**
Designed by Gianni Versace for his collection for spring/summer 1991, this printed silk evening dress features the faces of Marilyn Monroe and James Dean. It was first modelled on the catwalk by the supermodel, Naomi Campbell, and was inspired by the screenprints of Andy Warhol.

# The last sitting

However much her image has been rendered immortal over the years via art or advertising, the enduring memory of Marilyn—aside from on the cinema screen—was that captured by the myriad photographers who worked with her during her lifetime. The last time she was to pose for a photographic session was just six weeks before her death, with the commercial and fashion photographer Bert Stern. The New Yorker had been commissioned by *Vogue* magazine to shoot a feature in three sessions over two weeks at the Bel Air Hotel in suburban Los Angeles, starting on June 23, 1962.

Nearly 2,700 shots later, Stern's pictures—including fashion studies, portraits, and nudes—revealed a mature, confident and utterly sensual Marilyn; they showed a universal Marilyn whose humanity shone through, transcending the variety of "Marilyns" the world had been made familiar with over the years.

As a handful of other photographers had done before, though none would again, Stern captured the essential Marilyn—the quality that seemed to separate her from mere mortals. And, although her mortality would become only too apparent a month or so later, it was a quality that made her one of the immortals of recent times.

Marilyn Monroe is the first American goddess—our goddess of love… She is gone but she is everywhere. Stars die, but light goes on forever.

**Bert Stern**

421

# Photo Credits

**Mirrorpix**
p. 401

© **Ed Pfizenmaier**
pages 247, 248-249

**Rex Features**
pages 38, 74, 75, 113, 122, 153, 185, 205, 272, 336; **Bresler/Rex Features:** p. 43; **Peter Brooker/Rex Features:** pages 404, 407; **Peter Carrette/Rex Features:** p. 398; **Crollalanza/Rex Features:** p. 34; **Lewis Durham/Rex Features:** p. 406; **Everett Collection/Rex Features:** pages 5, 8, 68, 73, 78, 92, 204, 206, 217, 233, 303, 310, 332, 413; **Globe Photos Inc./Rex Features:** pages 41, 370; **IBL/Rex Features:** pages 322, 395; **Tony Kyriacou/Rex Features:** p. 419; **Media Press International/Rex Features:** p. 386–387; **Roger Viollet/Rex Features:** pages 219-219, 261, 340; **Sipa Press/Rex Features:** pages 15, 357, 390, 397, 421; **Sam Shaw/Rex Features:** pages 210-211, 225, 229, 230, 279, 282, 285, 286, 287, 288, 291; **Snap Photo Library/Rex Features:** pages 2, 16, 21, 27, 32, 33, 36, 37, 40, 44-45, 53, 54, 60, 61, 62, 63, 66, 70, 76-77, 80, 81, 83, 84-85, 89, 91, 93, 94, 96, 99, 100, 120, 103, 104, 105, 108, 109, 110, 112, 115, 116-117, 119, 120, 124, 129, 131, 133, 135, 139, 145, 147, 148, 154, 157, 165, 168, 171, 172, 173, 174-175, 179, 182, 184, 188-189, 191, 192, 200-201, 220, 221, 222, 224, 226-227, 238, 239, 258, 259, 276-277, 278, 281, 296-297, 308, 326-327, 330, 334, 335, 339, 343, 344, 360, 363, 364, 365, 373, 375, 385, 392, 417; **Stills/Rex Features:** p. 161

© **Bob Willoughby**
p. 325

# Quotation Credits

**CHAPTER 1**

p11  quoted in Donald Spoto *Marilyn Monroe: The Biography*, Chatto & Windus (UK) 1993, (hereafter referred to as Spoto) from Milton Greene archive

p12  talking to Michelle Morgan, The Marilyn Lives Society (UK) hereafter referred to as MLS

p13  David Conover, *Finding Marilyn*, Groset & Dunlap (US) 1981, hereafter referred to as Conover

p14  talking to George Belmont, *Marie Claire*, 1960

p17  quoted in *People* magazine, August 9, 1982

p23  *Sunday Express*, August 9, 1987

p25  MLS

p26a  James E. Dougherty, *The Secret Happiness of Marilyn Monroe*, Playboy Press (US)

p26b  MLS

p28  Conover

p30  Andrés de Dienes, *Marilyn*, Taschen 2002, hereafter referred to as AD

p32  quoted in "A Marilyn for all Seasons," *Life* magazine, July 1983

p35a  *Los Angeles Herald-Examiner*, August 7, 1962

p35b  Spoto

p36  AD

p39  AD

p41  quoted by Susan Bernard in *Bernard Of Hollywood*, Taschen 2002

p42a  "My Life with Young Marilyn," *Observer Magazine*, May 11, 1975

p42b  *Los Angeles Herald-Examiner*, August 7, 1962

**CHAPTER 2**

p51  quoted in *Marilyn and the Camera*, Bullfinch (US), 1989, hereafter referred to as MATC

p53  quoted in "The 1951 Model Blonde," Robert Cahn, *Colliers*, September 8, 1951

p 59  talking to Pete Martin, *Will Acting Spoil Marilyn Monroe?*, Doubleday, 1956

p61  quoted in Halliwell's *Who's Who In the Movies*, Harper Collins (UK) 1999

p62  quoted in Roger Taylor *Marilyn In Art*, Elm Tree/Hamish Hamilton (UK) 1984, hereafter referred to as Taylor

p69  Natasha Lytess, *Marilyn Monroe: Her Secret Life*, *The People*, July–August 1962

p72  *Los Angeles Daily News*, July 30, 1949

p79  quoted in www.marilynmonroe.com

p 82  quoted in MATC

p 93  talking in *The Legend Of Marilyn Monroe*, film documentary, David L. Wolper Productions 1964

p95  talking to Fred Lawrence Guiles, *Legend: TheLife and Death of Marilyn Monroe*, Scarborough House (US) 1992, hereafter referred to as Guiles

p111a  W.J. Weatherby, *Conversations With Marilyn*, Robson Books (UK) 1976

p111b  quoted in MATC

p114b  quoted in Guiles

p121  quoted in *Hollywood Studio Magazine*, August 1987

p125  Roy Ward Baker, *The Director's Cut*, Reynolds & Hearn (UK) 2000

p126  Rudy Behlmer, *Memo From Daryl F. Zanuck*, Grove Press (US) 1993

p131  *New York Herald Tribune*

p132  quoted in www.marilynmonroe.com

p134  *New York Post*, October 1952

p137  quoted in www.ellensplace.net/mquotes


## CHAPTER 3

p144  quoted in Adam Victor, *The Complete Marilyn Monroe*, Thames & Hudson (UK) 1999, hereafter referred to as Victor

p146  *New Yorker* magazine, January 1953

p149b  quoted in John Kobal, *People Will Talk*, Knopf (US) 1985

p 155  Joseph McBride, *Hawks On Hawks*, University of California Press (US) 1982

p156  quoted in Victor

p163  quoted in "Quotes said about Monroe" www.fortunecity.co.uk/cinerama

p164  Spoto

p169  Hearst newspapers, 1953

p170  quoted in www.marilynmonroe.com

p173  Otis L Guernsey, *New York Herald Tribune*, November 1953

p183  Bosley Crowther, *New York Times*, May 1954

p190  quoted in Guilles

p193  quoted in Victor

p202  quoted in "Marilyn Monroe Hits a New High," Robert Cahn, *Collier's*, 9 September 1954

p203  *MS* magazine, August 1972

p207  quoted in Victor


## CHAPTER 4

p213  press conference, 7 January 1955

p215  *Time* magazine, January 1956

p216  *Los Angeles Herald-Examiner*, August 5, 1982

p220  talking to Edward R Murrow/CBS *Person to Person*, April 8, 1955

p223  talking to Edward R Murrow/CBS *Person to Person*, April 8, 1955

p235  quoted in John Kobal, *People Will Talk*, Knopf (US) 1985

p240  quoted in *Victor*

p243  from "The Last Interview," www.royaturner.com

p245  Cecil Beaton, *The Restless Years: diaries 1955–1965*, Weidenfeld and Nicolson (UK) 1976

p250  Arthur Miller, *Timebends: A Life*, Methuen (US) 1987

p254  Arthur Miller, *Timebends: A Life*, Methuen (US) 1987

p260  quoted in "Quotations About Marilyn Monroe" at www.bellaonline.com

p263  *London Evening News*, July 15, 1956

p265  Justin Bowyer, *Conversations with Jack Cardiff*, BT Batsford (UK) 2003

p266a  Arthur Miller, *Timebends: A Life*, Methuen (US) 1987

p266b  *Time* magazine, August 6, 1956

p 268  Colin Clark, *The Prince, the Showgirl and Me*, Harper Collins (UK) 1995

p271  quoted MATC

p274  quoted in Una Pearl biography by Howard Mutti-Mewse on www.imdb.com

p279  quoted in Edward Wagenknecht, *Marilyn Monroe: A Composite View*, Chilton (US) 1969

p284  quoted in Spoto

p289  Arthur Miller, *Timebends: A Life*, Methuen (US) 1987

p290  quoted in Victor

p292  quoted in www.ellensplace.net/mquotes


**CHAPTER 5**

p298  to Spoto, November 19, 1991

p312  quoted in www.marilynmonroe.com

p315  Archer Winston, *New York Post*, April 1959

p328  Simone Signoret to press

p331a  quoted in Hervé Hamon/Patrick Rotman, Yves Montand: *Tu vois, je n'ai pas oublié*,
Seuil/Fayard, France 1990

p331b  MM at press reception, January 1960

p333  quoted in Ayn Rand "Through Your Most Grievous Fault," *Los Angeles Times*,
August 19, 1962

p338  John Huston, *An Open Book*, Knopf, US 1980

p341  quoted in www.marilynmonroe.com

p345b  *Variety*, February 1961

p345c  Paul V. Beckley, *New York Herald Tribune*, February 1961

p351  letter to Dr. Ralph Greenson 1/2 March 1961

p352  quoted in Taylor

p355  to Soto

p356  "Marilyn Monroe Quotes" in www.paralumun.com

p361  to Hollywood journalist Sheilah Graham

p368  to Spoto

p372  quoted in *New York Daily News*, May 20, 1962

p381  Gloria Steinem, *Marilyn*, Henry Holt (US) 1986


**CHAPTER 6**

p393  www.marilynmonroe.com

p394  quoted in "Famous Fans," www.penneylaing.freeserve.co.uk

p399  quoted in *Victor*

p400a  MLS

p400b  quoted in Haliwell's *Who's Who In The Movies*, Harper Collins (UK) 1999

p405  quoted in Taylor

p408  quoted in Taylor

p411 John Kobal, *Marilyn Monroe: A Life on Film*, Hamlyn (UK) 1974

p415 Andy Warhol and Pat Hackett, *POPism; the Warhol '60s*, Harper & Row (US) 1980

p418  quoted in Taylor

p420 Bert Stern, *The Last Sitting*, William Morrow (US) 1982

# BIBLIOGRAPHY

*Marilyn Monroe and the Camera*, Bullfinch (US), 1989

*The Directors Cut*, Roy Ward Baker, Reynolds & Hearn (UK), 2000

*The Restless Years: diaries 1955–1965*, Cecil Beaton, Weidenfeld and Nicolson,1976

*Memo From Daryl F. Zanuck*, Rudy Behlmer, Grove Press (US),1993

*Bernard Of Hollywood*, Susan Bernard, Taschen (Germany), 2002

*Conversations with Jack Cardiff*, Justin Bowyer, Batsford (UK), 2003

*The Prince, the Showgirl and Me*, Colin Clark, Harper Collins (UK), 1995

*Finding Marilyn*, David Conover, Groset & Dunlap (US), 1981

*Marilyn*, André de Dienes, Taschen (Germany), 2002

*The Secret Happiness of Marilyn Monroe*, James E. Dougherty, Playboy Press (US), 1976

*Legend: The Life and Death of Marilyn Monroe*, Fred Lawrence Guiles, Scarborough House (US), 1992

*Tu vois, je n'ai pas oublié*, Hervé Hamon/Patrick Rotman, Yves Montand: Seuil/Fayard, France 1990

*An Open Book*, John Huston, Knopf (US), 1980

*Marilyn Monroe*, John Kobal, Hamlyn (UK), 1974

*People Will Talk*, John Kobal, Knopf (US), 1985

*Marilyn: A Biography*, Norman Mailer, Hodder & Stoughton (UK), 1973

*Will Acting Spoil Marilyn Monroe?*, Pete Martin, Doubleday (US), 1956

*Hawks On Hawks*, Joseph McBride, University of California Press, 1982

*Timebends: A Life*, Arthur Miller, Methuen (US), 1987

*Striking Poses*, Richard Schickel, Pavilion (UK), 1987

*Marilyn Monroe: The Biography*, Donald Spoto, Chato and Windus (UK), 1992

*Marilyn*, Gloria Steinem, Henry Holt (US), 1986

*The Last Sitting*, Bert Stern, Morrow (US), 1982

*Marilyn In Art*, Roger G. Taylor, Elm Tree (UK), 1984

*New Biographical Dictionary of Film*, David Thomson, Little, Brown (UK), 2002

*The Complete Marilyn Monroe*, Adam Victor, Thames & Hudson (UK), 1999

*Marilyn Monroe: A Composite View*, Edward Wagenknecht, Chilton (US), 1969

*Conversations With Marilyn*, WJ Weatherby, Robson Books (UK), 1976

*The Show Business Nobody Knows*, Earl Wilson, Cowles Book Co (US), 1971

# Index

Page references in *italics* indicate illustration captions

First published by MQ Publications Limited
12 The Ivories
6–8 Northampton Street
London, N1 2HY
email: mqpublications.com
website: www.mqpublications.com

ISBN (10): 1-84072-674-1
ISBN (13): 978-1-84072-674-9

10 9 8 7 6 5 4 3 2

Printed in China